IRISH
WONDERS

"GOD SAVE YER HOLINESS." Frontispiece.

IRISH WONDERS

THE GHOSTS, GIANTS, POOKAS, DEMONS,
LEPRECHAWNS, BANSHEES, FAIRIES, WITCHES,
WIDOWS, AND OTHER MARVELS
OF THE EMERALD ISLE

POPULAR TALES AS TOLD BY THE PEOPLE

D. R. McANALLY, JR.

Illustrated by H. R. Heaton

GRAMERCY BOOKS
New York • Avenel

This 1996 edition is published by Gramercy Books,
a division of Random House Value Publishing, Inc.,
40 Engelhard Avenue, Avenel, New Jersey 07001.

Gramercy Books and colophon are trademarks of
Random House Value Publishing, Inc.

Random House
New York • Toronto • London • Sydney • Auckland
http://www.randomhouse.com/

Printed and bound in the United States of America

Library of Congress Cataloging-in-Publication Data
McAnally, David Rice, 1810-1895.
Irish Wonders: the ghosts, giants, pookas, demons, leprechawns, banshees, fairies,
witches, widows, old maids, and other marvels of the Emerald Isle: popular tales as told
by the people / D. R. McAnally; illustrated by H. R. Heaton
p. cm.
Originally published: Boston: Houghton Mifflin, 1888.
ISBN 0-517-12396-7
1. Tales—Ireland. 2. Folklore—Ireland. 3. Legends—Ireland.
4. Folk literature, Irish. 5. Mythology, Celtic. I. Heaton, H. R. II. Title
GR153.5.M38 1996
398.2'09415—dc20 96-2346 CIP

8 7 6 5 4 3 2 1

IN MEMORY OF YEARS OF FRIENDSHIP,

𝔗𝔥𝔦𝔰 𝔙𝔬𝔩𝔲𝔪𝔢

IS INSCRIBED TO

MR. JOSEPH B. McCULLAGH,

AS A MODEST TRIBUTE OF

PERSONAL RESPECT.

PREFACE.

THE wonderful imaginative power of the Celtic mind is never more strikingly displayed than in the legends and fanciful tales which people of the humbler walks of life seldom tire of telling. Go where you will in Ireland, the story-teller is there, and on slight provocation will repeat his narrative; amplifying, explaining, embellishing, till from a single fact a connected history is evolved, giving motives, particulars, action, and result, the whole surrounded by a rosy wealth of rustic imagery and told with dramatic force an actor might envy. The following chapters comprise an effort to present this phase of unwritten Celtic literature, the material having been collected during a recent lengthy visit, in the course of which every county in the island was traversed from end to end, and constant association had with the peasant tenantry. As, however, in perusing a drama each reader for himself supplies stage-action, so, in the following pages, he is requested to imagine the charms of gesticulation and intonation, for no pen can do justice to a story told by Irish lips amid Irish surroundings.

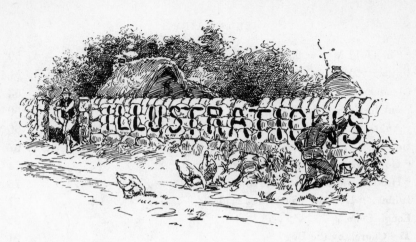

IRISH
WONDERS

THE SEVEN KINGS OF ATHENRY.

It was a characteristic Irish ruin. Standing on a slight elevation, in the midst of a flat country, the castle lifted its turreted walls as proudly as when its ramparts were fringed with banners and glittered with helmets and shields. In olden times it was the citadel of the town, and although Athenry was fortified by a strong wall, protecting it alike from predatory assault and organized attack, the citadel, occupying the highest ground within the city, was itself surrounded by stronger walls, a fort within a fort, making assurance of security doubly sure. Only by treachery, surprise, or regular and long-continued siege could the castle have been taken.

The central portion was a large, square structure; except in size, not differing greatly from the isolated castles found in all parts of Ireland, and always in pairs, as if, when one Irish chieftain built a castle, his rival at once erected another a mile or so away, for the purpose of holding him in check. This central fort was connected by double walls, the remains of

covered passages, with smaller fortresses, little castles built
into the wall surrounding the citadel ; and over these connect-
ing walls, over the little castles, and over the piles of loose
stones where once the strong outer walls had stood, the ivy
grew in luxuriant profusion, throwing its dark green curtain
on the unsightly masses, rounding the sharp edge of the masonry, hiding the rough corners as though ashamed of their
roughness, and climbing the battlements of the central castle
to spread nature's mantle of charity over the remains of a
barbarous age, and forever conceal from human view the
stony reminders of battle and blood.

The success of the ivy was not complete. Here and there
the corner of a battlement stood out in sharp relief, as though
it had pushed back the struggling plant, and, by main force,
had risen above the leaves, while on one side a round tower
lifted itself as if to show that a stone tower could stand for
six hundred years without permitting itself to become ivy-
grown ; that there could be individuality in towers as among
men. The great arched gateway too was not entirely subju-
gated, though the climbing tendrils and velvety leaves dressed
the pillars and encroached on the arch. The keystone bore
a rudely carved, crowned head, and ivy vines, coming up un-
derneath the arch, to take the old king by surprise, climbed
the bearded chin, crossed the lips, and were playing before the
nose as if to give it a sportive tweak, while the stern brow
frowned in anger at the plant's presumption.

But only a few surly crags of the citadel refused to go
gracefully into the retirement furnished by the ivy, and the
loving plant softened every outline, filled up every crevice,
bridged the gaps in the walls, toned down the rudeness of
projecting stones, and did everything that an ivy-plant could
do to make the rugged old castle as presentable as were the

high rounded mounds without the city, cast up by the besiegers when the enemy last encamped against it.

The old castle had fallen on evil days, for around the walls of the citadel clustered the miserable huts of the modern Irish village. The imposing castle gate faced a lane, muddy and foul with the refuse thrown from the houses. The ivy-man-

tled towers looked down upon earth and stone huts, with thatched roofs, low chimneys, and doors seeming as if the builder designed them for windows and changed his mind without altering their size, but simply continued them to the ground and made them answer the purpose. A population, notable chiefly for its numerousness and lack of cleanliness,

presented itself at every door, but little merriment was heard
in the alleys of Athenry.

"Sure it's mighty little they have to laugh at," said the
car-man. "Indade, the times has changed fur the counthry,
Sorr. Wanst Ireland was as full o' payple as a Dublin
sthrate, an' they was all as happy as a grazin' colt, an' as
paceful as a basket av puppies, barrin' a bit o' fun at a marryin' or a wake, but thim times is all gone. Wid the landlords, an' the guver'mint, an' the sojers, an' the polis, lettin'
in the rich an' turnin' out the poor, Irishmin is shtarvin' to
death. See that bit av a cabin there, Sorr? Sure there's
foorteen o' thim in it, an' two pigs, an' tin fowls; they all
shlape togather on a pile av wet shtraw in the corner, an'
sorra a wan o' thim knows where the bit in the mornin' is to
come from. Phat do they ate? They're not in the laste pur-
tickler. Spakin' ginerally, whatever they can get. They've
pitaties an' milk, an' sometimes pitaties an' no milk, an' av a
Sunday a bit o' mate that's a herrin', an' not a boot to the
fut o' thim, an' they paddlin' in the wather on the flure. Sure
the town's full o' thim an' the likes av thim. Begorra, the
times has changed since the siven Kings held coort in the castle beyant yon.

"Niver heard o' the Siven Kings av Athenroy? Why ivery
babby knows the whole shtory be heart, an' all about thim.
Faith I'll tell it, fur it's not desayvin' ye I am, fur the ould
castle was wan o' the greatest places in the counthry.

"Wanst upon a time, there was an ould King in Athenroy,
that, be all accounts, was the besht ould King that iver set
fut upon a throne. He was a tall ould King, an' the hairs av
him an' the beard av him was as white as a shnow-flake, an' he
had a long, grane dressin' gown, wid shamrocks av goold all
over it, an' a goold crown as high as a gintleman's hat, wid a

dimund as big as yer fisht on the front av it, an' silver shlippers
on the feet av him. An' he had grane cârpets on the groun'
in the hall o' the ould castle, an' begob, they do say that
everything about the coort was goold, but av that I'm not
rightly sartain, barrin' the pipe. That was av goold, bekase
there's a picture av him hangin' in Michael Flaherty's shebeen,
an' the pipe is just the look av goold an' so it must have been.

  "An' he was the besht King in Ireland, an' sorra a beggar
'ud come an the dure, but the King 'ud come out in his
gown an' shlippers an' ax him how he come to be poor, an'
sind him 'round to the kitchen to be warrumed wid a dhrop
av whishkey an' fed wid all the cold pitaties that was in the
panthry. All the people riz up whin he was a-walkin' down
the shtrate wid a big goold-top shtick in his hand, an' the
crown a-shinin' on his head, an' they said, 'God save yer Holiness,' an' he said, 'God save ye kindly,' mighty perlite, bekase he was a dacent mannered ould King, an' 'ud shpake to
a poor divil that had n't a coat on his back as quick as to wan
av his ginerals wid a goold watch an' a shiny hat. An' whin
he wint into a shop, sure they niver axed him to show the
color av his money at all, but the man 'ud say, 'God save ye!
Sure ye can pay whin ye plaze, an' I'll sind it be the postman
whin he goes by.' An' the ould King 'ud say, 'Oh, I wont
throuble ye. Bedad, I'll carry it,' an' aff the blessed ould
King 'ud go, wid his bundles undher his arm, an' the crown
on his head, as happy as a widdy wid a new husband.

  "An' there was six other ould Kings, that was frinds to
him, an' they was all as like him as six paze. Foor times a
year they'd all come to Athenroy fur a bit av a shpree like,
bekase the King av Athenroy was the ouldest av thim, an' they
thought the worruld an' all av him. Faix, it was mighty
improvin' to see thim all a-goin' to chapel in the mornin',

an' singin' an' drinkin' an' playin' whisht in the avenin'. Sure thim was the blessed days fur the counthry.

"Well me dear, in coorse av time, the six ould Kings all died, God rest their sowls, but as aitch wan had a son to come afther him, the differ was mighty shmall, for the young Kings was dacent shpoken lads an' kept on comin' to Athenroy just like the ould Kings.

"Oh, bedad, I forgot to tell yez that the ould King had a dawther, that was the light av his eyes. She was as tall as a sargent an' as shtrate as a gun, an' her eyes was as blue as the shky an' shone like the shtars. An' her hairs was t'reads av goold, an' she was the beautifulest woman iver seen in Athenroy. An' shmall love there was for her, fur she was as cowld as a wet Christmas. She did n't shpake often, bekase she was n't wan o' thim that 'ud deefen a smith, but whin she did, the tongue that was in the head av her was like a sting-nettle, an' 'ud lash around like a throut on land. An' ivery woman in the shtrate watched her like kites whin she set fut out o' the dure, bekase she dressed as fine as a fiddle, wid a grane silk gown, an' a blue bonnet wid yellow ribbins, an' a shtring av goold baids the size av plums 'round her neck.

"Musha, thin, it's a quare thing entirely, that min like wan woman betther than another. Begob, it's my belafe, savin' yer prisence, that there's not the differ av a cowld pitaty bechune thim all whin it's a queshtion av marryin' wan o' thim, an' if the whole worruld knewn that same, its few hurted heads there'd be along o' the wimmin. Well, it was the divil's own job, axin' yer pardon, but ivery wan o' thim young Kings tuk into his head to fall in love wid the Princess Bridget, fur that was her name, an' a good name it is; an' wan afther another, they'd shlip in whin they'd be passin', to pay their respicts. Whin wan o' thim found out that another wan was comin', he'd come the aftener himself to make up fur it, an' afther a while, they all found out aitch other, an' thin, begob all o' thim come to be beforehand wid the rest, an' from foor times in the year, it was foor times in

the week that the gang o' them 'ud be settin' in the kitchen till the cock 'ud crow, all a-makin' love to the young Princess.

" An' a fine sight it was to see thim, bekase they was all shtrivin' to do somethin' for her. Whin she paled the pitaties fur the ould King's brekquest, sure wan o' thim 'ud be givin' her the pitaties, another wan 'ud catch the palin' an' the rest lookin' on wid the invy shinin' out o' their faces.

Whin she dropped the thimble, you'd think the last wan 'ud jump out av his shkin to get it, an' whin she wint to milk the cow, wan 'ud carry the pail, another wan 'ud fetch the shtool, an' two 'ud feed the cow, an' two other wans 'ud hold the calf, an' aitch wan 'ud bless God whin she gev him the laste shmile, bekase she was so cowld, d' ye mind, that divil a wan o' thim all cud say that he'd get her at all.

" So at firsht, ould King Dennis, that bein' his name, was mighty plazed to see the young chaps all afther his dawther, an' whin he knewn they was in the kitchen, he'd shmoke his pipe an' have his sup be himself in the other room so as to lave thim ; an' whin he saw thim hangin' over the wall o' the gârden beyant, or peepin' through the hedge, he'd let on not to parsave thim ; an' whin they folly'd the Princess to church, he was as proud as a paycock to see thim settin' behind her wid their crowns in a row undher the sate. But whin they kept an a-comin' ivery night in the week an' drinkin' his whishkey an' shmokin' his besht terbakky, — more-betoken, whin they begun' to be oncivil to aitch other, says he to himself, says he, ' Bedad,' says he, ' there'll be throuble if it kapes on thish-a-way. Sure I'll shpake to the gurrul.'

" So he called to the Princess, ' Biddy,' says he.

" ' What, Father ?' says she.

" ' Come here to me,' says he.

" ' Sure how can I ? I 'm busy,' says she.

" ' Phat 's that you 're at ? ' says he.

" ' I 'm afther shwapin' the kitchen,' says she.

" ' Lave aff,' says he. ' Come to me at wanst,' says he.

" The ould King was very starn, bekase he knewn it was only an axcuse she was afther makin,' an' she was lookin' that he'd be sayin' somethin' about the young Kings an' was afther dodgin' as long as she cud. So whin he shpoke so

crass, she riz up aff the sate, for it was a fib she was tellin',
an' she did n't shwape the kitchen at all, an' that was done
be wan av the maids, an' gev a sigh, an' wint in the ould
King's room.

"An' there was the ould King on his throne, his crown
on his head, shmokin' his goolden dhudeen wid a glass o'
grog at his side, as detarmined as he cud be. 'I 'm wantin'
to know,' says he, 'phat you 're afther goin' to do,' says he,
'in regârds av the young Kings,' says he.

"'Phat 's that you 're sayin', Father?' says she, mighty
shly, as lettin' on not to see phat he was drivin' at. The ould
King repated his statemint.

"'Troth, then, I dunno, Father,' says she.

"'Do you mane to marry thim, at all, at all?' says he.

"'Not all o' thim,' says she, shmilin'.

"'Well, which wan o' thim?' says he.

"'How can I tell?' says she.

"'Has any o' thim axed ye?' says he.

"'Has n't they all?' says she.

"'An' which wan do ye love besht?' says he.

"'Sure how do I know?' says she, an' sorra a word more
cud he get from her be all the queshtions he cud ax.

"But he tuk a dale av bother an' thin gev it up an' says to
her, 'Go an' get the supper,' says he, 'come in the throne-
room afther brekquest wid yer mind made.' But he was
afeard she 'd give him throuble fur it was the cool face she
had, an' afther she was gone he set his crown over wan ear
an' scrotched his head like a tinant on quarther day widout
a pinny in his pocket, bekase he knewn that whoever the
gurrul tuk, the other five Kings cud make throuble.

"So the next mornin', the Princess towld him phat she 'd
do, an' whin the Kings come that night, he walks into the

kitchen where they were shmokin', an' makin' a low bow, he
says, ' God save ye,' an' they all riz an' says, ' God save yer
Holiness.' So he says, ' Bridget, go to bed immejitly, I 'll
shpake to the jintlemin.' An' she wint away, lettin' an to
shmile an' consale her face, 't was the divil av a sharp gurrul
she was, an' the ould King set on the table an' towld thim
phat she 'd do. He towld thim they must play fair, an' they
said they would, an' thin he towld thim the Princess wanted
to see which was the besht man, so they must have shports
in her prisence, an' the next day afther the shports they 'd
find out who she was goin' to marry. So they all aggrade,
an' wint home at wanst to get ready fur the shports.

" Faith, it 'ud 'uv done the sowl av ye good the next day
to see the whole av Ireland at the shports whin the contist
bechune the Kings kem.

" 'T was held in the field beyant, an' they made a ring an'
the six young Kings run races an' rassled an' played all the
axcitin' games that was iver knewn, aitch wid wan eye on the
shports an' the other on the Princess, that was shmilin' an
thim all an' lookin' as plazed as a new Mimber o' Parlaymint,
an' so did they all, bekase, d' ye see, before the shports begun,
they was brought, wan at a time, in the coort, an' the Princess talked wid aitch be himself, was n't it the shly purtinder
that she was, fur whin they kem out, every wan was shmilin'
to himself, as fur to say he had a very agrayble saycret.

" So the shports was ended an' everybody wint home,
barrin' thim as shtopped at the shebeens. But sorra a wink
o' shlape crassed the eyes av wan o' the young Kings, fur
the joy that was in the heart o' thim, bekase aitch knewn
he 'd get the Princess.

" Whin the mornin' come, the like o' the flusthration that
was in Athenroy was niver seen afore, nor sense aither, fur

"DIVIL A WAN O' ME KNOWS," SAYS HE. Page 13.

whin the maid wint to call the Princess, sure she was n't there. So they sarched the coort from the garret to the cellar an' peeped in the well an' found she was nowhere entirely.

"So they towld the ould King, an' says he, 'Baithershin, where is she at all,' says he, 'an' phat 'ull I be sayin' to the young Kings whin they come.' An' there he was, a-tarin' the long white hair av him, whin the young Kings all come.

" 'God save yer Holiness,' says they to him.

" 'God save ye kindly,' says he, fur wid all the sorra that was in him, sure he did n't forgit to be perlite, bekase he was as cunnin' as a fox, an' knewn he 'd nade all his good manners to make aminds fur his dawther's absince. So, says he, 'God save ye kindly,' says he, bowin'.

" 'An' where is the Princess?' says they.

" 'Divil a wan o' me knows,' says he.

" 'Sure it 's jokin' wid us ye are,' says the Kings.

" 'Faix, I 'm not,' says the ould King. 'Bad cess to the thrace av her was seen sense she went to bed.'

" 'Sure she did n't go to bed entirely,' says the maid, 'the bed was n't touched, an' her besht gown 's gone.'

" 'An' where has she gone?' says the Kings.

" 'Tare an' 'ounds,' says the ould King, 'am n't I ignerant entirely? Och, Biddy, Biddy, how cud ye sarve me so?' a-wringing his hands wid the graif.

"Well, at firsht the Kings looked at aitch other as if the eyes 'ud lave thim, bein' all dazed like an' sarcumvinted intirely. An' thin they got their wits about thim, an' begun to be angry.

" 'It 's desayvin' us ye are, ye outprobious ould villin,' says they to him. 'Musha, thin, bad cess to ye, bring out the Princess an' let her make her chice bechune us, or it 'll be the worse fur ye, ye palaverin' ould daddy long-legs,' says they.

" ' God bechune us an' harm,' says the ould King, ' sure d' ye think it 's makin' fun av ye I am, an' me spindin' more than tin pounds yestherday fur whishkey an the shports? Faix, she 's gone,' says he.

" ' Where to ? ' says they.

" ' Divil a know I know,' says he, wid the face av him gettin' red, an' wid that word they all wint away in a tarin' rage wid him, fur they consaved, an' shmall blame to thim, that he had her consaled in the coort an' was shtrivin' to chate thim.

" An' they wint home an' got their armies, an' come back wid 'em that night, an' while the ould King an' his min were all ashlape they made these piles av airth to take the city whin the day 'ud break.

" Whin the ould King riz an' tuk a walk an the roof wid his shlippers, sure phat 'ud he see but banners a-wavin', soords a-flashin', an' the ears av him was deefened wid the thrumpets. ' Bad scran to the idjits,' says he ; ' phat 's that they 're afther ? ' says he. ' Is n't there more nor wan woman in the worruld, that they 're makin' a bother afther Bridget ? ' So wid that he ordhered his min to get ready wid their waypons, an' before the battle 'ud begin, he wint out to thry an' make a thraty.

" While they were a-talkin', up comes wan av the King's tinants, wid a donkey an' a load av sayweed fur the King's gârden, that he 'd been to Galway afther. ' God save ye,' says he, a-touchin' his cap ; ' where is the six Kings? '

" ' An' phat d' ye want, ye blaggârd? ' says they, lookin' lofty.

" ' I 've a message fur yez,' says he, ' from the young Princess,' an' whin they heard him shpake, they all stopped to listen.

" ' She sent her respicts,' says he, ' an' bid me tell yez that she was afther kapin' her word an' lettin' yer Honors know who she was goin' to marry. It 's the King av Galway that 's in it, if it 's plazin' to ye, an' she says she 'll sind yez a bit av the cake. I met her lasht night in the road ridin' wid him on a câr an' had a bundle undher her arrum. Divil a taste av a lie 's in it entirely.'

"Bad cess to the gurrul, it was thrue fur him, fur she had run away. But, my dear, it was as good as the theayter to see the six young Kings an' the ould King, a-lookin' at aitch other as stupid as a jackass, all as wan as the castle 'ad 'a'

fallen on thim. But they was sinsible young fellys, an' seen the Princess had desaved thim all complately.

"'Bad scran to the gurrul,' says they, 'an' it 's the blessed fools we was fur belavin' her.' Thin they come to talk to aitch other, an' wan says, 'Sure she thought most av me, fur she towld me she hoped I 'd bate yez,' says he. 'Begob, she said to me that same,' says the other wans, an' they stud, scrotchin' the heads av thim an' disconsarted intirely.

"'An' phat 's the good av fightin',' says the ould King, 'bein' as we 're all in the thrap at wanst?'

"'Thrue fur ye,' says they. 'We 'll dispinse widout her. We 'll have it out wid the King o' Galway,' says they.

"An' they all wint into the coort an' had the bit an' sup, an' made a thraty forninst the King av Galway. It was the great war that was in it, the Siven Kings wid the King av Galway, an' bate him out o' the counthry intirely. But it's my consate that they was all fools to be afther fightin' consarnin' wan woman whin the worruld is full o' thim, an' any wan competint to give a man plenty to think av, bekase whin she gives her attinshun to it, any woman can be the divil complately."

TAMING THE POOKA.

HE west and northwest coast of Ireland shows many remarkable geological formations, but, excepting the Giant's Causeway, no more striking spectacle is presented than that to the south of Galway Bay. From the sea, the mountains rise in terraces like gigantic stairs, the layers of stone being apparently harder and denser on the upper surfaces than beneath, so the lower portion of each layer, disintegrating first, is washed away by the rains and a clearly defined step is formed. These terraces are generally about twenty feet high, and of a breadth, varying with the situation and exposure, of from ten to fifty feet.

The highway from Ennis to Ballyvaughn, a fishing village opposite Galway, winds, by a circuitous course, through these freaks of nature, and, on the long descent from the high land to the sea level, passes the most conspicuous of the neighboring mountains, the Corkscrew Hill. The general shape of the mountain is conical, the terraces composing it are of wonderful regularity from the base to the peak, and the strata being

sharply upturned from the horizontal, the impression given is
that of a broad road carved out of the sides of the mountain
and winding by an easy ascent to the summit.

"'T is the Pooka's Path they call it," said the car-man.
"Phat's the Pooka? Well, that's not aisy to say. It's an
avil sper't that does be always in mischief, but sure it niver
does sarious harrum axceptin' to thim that desarves it, or thim
that shpakes av it disrespictful. I never seen it, Glory be to
God, but there's thim that has, and be the same token, they
do say that it looks like the finest black horse that iver wore
shoes. But it is n't a horse at all at all, for no horse 'ud have
eyes av fire, or be breathin' flames av blue wid a shmell o'
sulfur, savin' yer presince, or a shnort like thunder, and no
mortial horse 'ud take the lapes it does, or go as fur widout
gettin' tired. Sure when it give Tim O'Bryan the ride it give
him, it wint from Gort to Athlone wid wan jump, an' the next
it tuk he was in Mullingyar, and the next was in Dublin, and
back agin be way av Kilkenny an' Limerick, an' niver turned
a hair. How far is that? Faith I dunno, but it's a power
av distance, an' clane acrost Ireland an' back. He knew it
was the Pooka bekase it shpake to him like a Christian mortial,
only it is n't agrayble in its language an' 'ull niver give ye a
dacint word afther ye're on its back, an' sometimes not before
aither.

"Sure Dennis O'Rourke was afther comin' home wan night,
it was only a boy I was, but I mind him tellin' the shtory, an'
it was at a fair in Galway he'd been. He'd been havin' a
sup, some says more, but whin he come to the rath, and jist
beyant where the fairies dance and ferninst the wall where the
polisman was shot last winther, he fell in the ditch, quite spint
and tired complately. It was n't the length as much as the
wideness av the road was in it, fur he was goin' from wan side

to the other an' it was too much fur him entirely. So he laid
shtill fur a bit and thin thried fur to get up, but his legs wor
light and his head was heavy, an' whin he attimpted to get his
feet an the road 't was his head that was an it, bekase his legs
cud n't balance it. Well, he laid there and was bet entirely,
an' while he was studyin' how he 'd raise, he heard the throt-
tin' av a horse on the road.   ' 'T is meself 'ull get the lift
now,' says he, and laid waitin', and up comes the Pooka.   Whin

Dennis seen him, begob, he kivered his face wid his hands
and turned on the breast av him, and roared wid fright like a
bull.

"' Arrah thin, ye snakin' blaggârd,' says the Pooka, mighty
short, 'lave aff yer bawlin' or I 'll kick ye to the ind av next
week,' says he to him.

"But Dennis was scairt, an' bellered louder than afore, so
the Pooka, wid his hoof, give him a crack on the back that
knocked the wind out av him.

" 'Will ye lave aff,' says the Pooka, 'or will I give ye another, ye roarin' dough-face?'

" Dennis left aff blubberin' so the Pooka got his timper back.

" 'Shtand up, ye guzzlin' sarpint,' says the Pooka, 'I 'll give ye a ride.'

" 'Plaze yer Honor,' says Dennis, 'I can't. Sure I 've not been afther drinkin' at all, but shmokin' too much an' atin', an' it 's sick I am, and not ontoxicated.'

" 'Och, ye dhrunken buzzard,' says the Pooka, 'Don't offer fur to desave me,' liftin' up his hoof agin, an' givin' his tail a swish that sounded like the noise av a catheract, 'Did n't I thrack ye for two miles be yer breath,' says he, 'An' you shmellin' like a potheen fact'ry,' says he, 'an' the nose on yer face as red as a turkey-cock's. Get up, or I 'll lift ye,' says he, jumpin' up an' cracking his hind fut like he was doin' a jig.

" Dennis did his best, an' the Pooka helped him wid a grip o' the teeth on his collar.

" 'Pick up yer caubeen,' says the Pooka, 'an' climb up. I 'll give ye such a ride as ye niver dhramed av.'

" 'Ef it 's plazin' to yer Honor,' says Dennis, 'I 'd laver walk. Ridin' makes me dizzy,' says he.

" ' 'T is not plazin',' says the Pooka, 'will ye get up or will I kick the shtuffin' out av yer cowardly carkidge,' says he, turnin' round an' flourishin' his heels in Dennis' face.

" Poor Dennis thried, but he cud n't, so the Pooka tuk him to the wall an' give him a lift an it, an' whin Dennis was mounted, an' had a tight howld on the mane, the first lep he give was down the rock there, a thousand feet into the field ye see, thin up agin, an' over the mountain, an' into the say, an' out agin, from the top av the waves to the top av the mountain, an' afther the poor soggarth av a ditcher was nigh onto dead, the Pooka come back here wid him an' dhropped him in the ditch where he found him, an' blowed in his face to put him to slape, so lavin' him. An' they found Dennis in the mornin' an' carried him home, no more cud he walk for a fortnight be razon av the wakeness av his bones fur the ride he 'd had.

"But sure, the Pooka 's a different baste entirely to phat he was afore King Bryan-Boru tamed him. Niver heard av him? Well, he was the king av Munster an' all Ireland an' tamed the Pooka wanst fur all on the Corkschrew Hill fer-ninst ye.

"Ye see, in the owld days, the counthry was full av avil sper'ts, an' fairies an' witches, an' divils entirely, and the harrum they done was onsaycin', for they wor always comin' an' goin', like Mulligan's blanket, an' widout so much as sayin', by yer lave. The fairies 'ud be dancin' on the grass every night be the light av the moon, an' stalin' away the childhre, an' many 's the wan they tuk that niver come back. The owld rath on the hill beyant was full av the dead, an' afther night-fall they 'd come from their graves an' walk in a long line wan afther another to the owld church in the valley where they 'd go in an' stay till cock-crow, thin they 'd come out agin an' back to the rath. Sorra a parish widout a witch, an' some nights they 'd have a great enthertainmint on the Corkschrew Hill, an' you 'd see thim, wid shnakes on their arrums an' necks an' ears, be way av jewels, an' the eyes av dead men in their hair, comin' for miles an' miles, some ridin' through the air on shticks an' bats an' owls, an' some walkin', an' more on Pookas an' horses wid wings that 'ud come up in line to the top av the hill, like the cabs at the dure o' the theayter, an' lave thim there an' hurry aff to bring more.

"Sometimes the Owld Inimy, Satan himself, 'ud be there at the enthertainmint, comin' an a monsthrous draggin, wid grane shcales an' eyes like the lightnin' in the heavens, an' a roarin' fiery mouth like a lime-kiln. It was the great day thin, for they do say all the witches brought their rayports at thim saysons fur to show him phat they done.

"Some 'ud tell how they shtopped the wather in a spring, an' inconvanienced the nabers, more 'ud show how they dhried the cow's milk, an' made her kick the pail, an' they'd all laugh like to shplit. Some had blighted the corn, more had brought the rains on the harvest. Some towld how their enchantmints made the childhre fall ill, some said how they set the thatch on fire, more towld how they shtole the eggs, or spiled the crame in the churn, or bewitched the butther so it'ud n't come, or led the shape into the bog. But that was n't all.

"Wan 'ud have the head av a man murthered be her manes, an' wid it the hand av him hung fur the murther; wan 'ud bring the knife she'd scuttled a boat wid an' pint in the say to where the corpses laid av the fishermen she'd dhrownded; wan 'ud carry on her breast the child she'd shtolen an' meant to bring up in avil, an' another wan 'ud show the little white body av a babby she'd smothered in its slape. And the corpse-candles 'ud tell how they desaved the thraveller, bringin' him to the river, an' the avil sper'ts 'ud say how they dhrew him in an' down to the bottom in his sins an' thin to the pit wid him. An' owld Belzebub 'ud listen to all av thim, wid a rayporther, like thim that's afther takin' down the spaches at a Lague meetin', be his side, a-writing phat they said, so as whin they come to be paid, it 'ud n't be forgotten.

"Thim wor the times fur the Pookas too, fur they had power over thim that wint forth afther night, axceptin' it was on an arriant av marcy they were. But sorra a sinner that had n't been to his juty reglar 'ud iver see the light av day agin afther meetin' a Pooka thin, for the baste 'ud aither kick him to shmithereens where he stud, or lift him on his back wid his teeth an' jump into the say wid him, thin dive, lavin' him to dhrownd, or shpring over a clift wid him an' tumble him to the bottom a bleedin' corpse. But was n't there the howls av joy whin a Pooka 'ud catch a sinner unbeknownst, an' fetch him on the Corkschrew wan o' the nights Satan was there. Och, God defind us, phat a sight it was. They made a ring wid the corpse-candles, while the witches tore him limb from limb, an' the fiends drunk his blood in red-hot iron noggins wid shrieks o' laughter to smother his schreams, an' the Pookas jumped on his body an' thrampled it into the ground, an' the timpest 'ud whishle a chune, an' the mountains about 'ud kape time, an' the Pookas, an' witches, an' sper'ts av avil, an' corpse-candles, an' bodies o' the dead, an' divils, 'ud all jig together round the rock where owld Belzebub 'ud set shmilin', as fur to say he 'd ax no betther divarshun. God's presince be wid us, it makes me crape to think av it.

"Well, as I was afther sayin', in the time av King Bryan, the Pookas done a dale o' harrum, but as thim that they murthered wor dhrunken bastes that wor in the shebeens in the day an' in the ditch be night, an' was n't missed whin the Pookas tuk them, the King paid no attintion, an' small blame to him that 's.

"But wan night, the queen's babby fell ill, an' the king says to his man, says he, 'Here, Riley, get you up an' on the white mare an' go fur the docther.'

" ' Musha thin,' says Riley, an' the king's counthry house was in the break o' the hills, so Riley 'ud pass the rath an' the Corkschrew on the way afther the docther; 'Musha thin,' says he, aisey and on the quiet, 'it 's mesilf that does n't want that same job.'

"So he says to the king, 'Won't it do in the mornin'?'

"'It will not,' says the king to him. 'Up, ye lazy beggar, atin' me bread, an' the life lavin' me child.'

"So he wint, wid great shlowness, tuk the white mare, an' aff, an' that was the last seen o' him or the mare aither, fur the Pooka tuk 'em. Sorra a taste av a lie 's in it, for thim that said they seen him in Cork two days afther, thrading aff the white mare, was desaved be the sper'ts, that made it seem to be him whin it was n't that they 've a thrick o' doin'.

"Well, the babby got well agin, bekase the docther did n't get there, so the king left botherin' afther it and begun to wondher about Riley an' the white mare, and sarched fur thim but did n't find thim. An' thin he knewn that they was gone entirely, bekase, ye see, the Pooka did n't lave as much as a hair o' the mare's tail.

"'Wurra thin,' says he, 'is it horses that the Pooka 'ull be stalin'? Bad cess to its impidince! This 'ull niver do. Sure we 'll be ruinated entirely,' says he.

"Mind ye now, it 's my consate from phat he said, that the king was n't consarned much about Riley, fur he knewn that he cud get more Irishmen whin he wanted thim, but phat he meant to say was that if the Pooka tuk to horse-stalin', he 'd be ruinated entirely, so he would, for where 'ud he get another white mare? So it was a mighty sarious question an' he retired widin himself in the coort wid a big book that he had that towld saycrets. He 'd a sight av larnin', had the king, aquel to a school-masther, an' a head that 'ud sarcumvint a fox.

"So he read an' read as fast as he cud, an' afther readin' widout shtoppin', barrin' fur the bit an' sup, fur siven days

an' nights, he come out, an' whin they axed him cud he bate
the Pooka now, he said niver a word, axceptin' a wink wid his
eye, as fur to say he had him.

"So that day he was in the fields an' along be the hedges
an' ditches from sunrise to sunset, collectin' the matarials av a
dose fur the Pooka, but phat he got, faith, I dunno, no more
does any wan, fur he never said, but kep the saycret to himself
an' did n't say it aven to the quane, fur he knewn that saycrets
run through a woman like wather in a ditch. But there was
wan thing about it that he cud n't help tellin', fur he wanted

it but cud n't get it widout help, an' that was three hairs from the Pooka's tail, axceptin' which the charm 'ud n't work. So he towld a man he had, he 'd give him no end av goold if he 'd get thim fur him, but the felly pulled aff his caubeen an' scrotched his head an' says, ' Faix, yer Honor, I dunno phat 'll be the good to me av the goold if the Pooka gets a crack at me carkidge wid his hind heels,' an' he wud n't undhertake the job on no wages, so the king begun to be afeared that his loaf was dough.

" But it happen'd av the Friday, this bein' av a Chewsday, that the Pooka caught a sailor that had n't been on land only long enough to get bilin' dhrunk, an' got him on his back, so jumped over the clift wid him lavin' him dead enough, I go bail. Whin they come to sarch the sailor to see phat he had in his pockets, they found three long hairs round the third button av his top-coat. So they tuk thim to the king tellin' him where they got thim, an' he was greatly rejiced, bekase now he belaved he had the Pooka sure enough, so he ended his inchantmint.

" But as the avenin' come, he riz a doubt in the mind av him thish-a-way. Ev the three hairs wor out av the Pooka's tail, the charm 'ud be good enough, but if they was n't, an' was from his mane inshtead, or from a horse inshtead av a Pooka, the charm 'ud n't work an' the Pooka 'ud get atop av him wid all the feet he had at wanst an' be the death av him immejitly. So this nate and outprobrious argymint shtruck the king wid great force an' fur a bit, he was onaisey. But wid a little sarcumvintion, he got round it, for he confist an' had absolu- tion so as he 'd be ready, thin he towld wan av the sarvints to come in an' tell him afther supper, that there was a poor widdy in the boreen beyant the Corkschrew that wanted help that night, that it 'ud be an arriant av marcy he 'd be on, an' so safe agin the Pooka if the charm did n't howld.

" ' Sure, phat 'll be the good o' that ? ' says the man, ' It 'ull be a lie, an' won't work.'

" ' Do you be aisey in yer mind,' says the king to him agin, ' do as yer towld an' don't argy, for that 's a pint av metty-fisics,' says he, faix it was a dale av deep larnin' he had, ' that 's a pint av mettyfisics an' the more ye argy on thim subjics, the less ye know,' says he, an' it 's thrue fur him. ' Besides, aven if it 's a lie, it 'll desave the Pooka, that 's no mettyfishian, an' it 's my belafe that the end is good enough for the manes,' says he, a-thinking av the white mare.

" So, afther supper, as the king was settin' afore the fire, an' had the charm in his pocket, the sarvint come in and towld him about the widdy.

" ' Begob,' says the king, like he was surprised, so as to desave the Pooka complately, ' Ev that 's thrue, I must go relave her at wanst.' So he riz an' put on sojer boots, wid shpurs on 'em a fut acrost, an' tuk a long whip in his hand, for fear, he said, the widdy 'ud have dogs, thin wint to his chist an' tuk his owld stockin' an' got a suv'rin out av it, — Och, 't was the shly wan he was, to do everything so well, — an' wint out wid his right fut first, an' the shpurs a-rattlin' as he walked.

" He come acrost the yard, an' up the hill beyant yon an' round the corner, but seen nothin' at all. Thin up the fut path round the Corkscrew an' met niver a sowl but a dog that he cast a shtone at. But he did n't go out av the road to the widdy's, for he was afeared that if he met the Pooka an' he caught him in a lie, not bein' in the road to where he said he was goin,' it 'ud be all over wid him. So he walked up an' down bechuxt the owld church below there an' the rath on the hill, an' jist as the clock was shtrikin' fur twelve, he heard a horse in front av him, as he was walkin' down, so

he turned an' wint the other way, gettin' his charm ready, an'
the Pooka come up afther him.

"'The top o' the mornin' to yer Honor,' says the Pooka,
as perlite as a Frinchman, for he seen be his close that the
king was n't a common blaggârd like us, but was wan o' the
rale quolity.

"'Me sarvice to ye,' says the king to him agin, as bowld as
a ram, an' whin the Pooka heard him shpake, he got perliter
than iver, an' made a low bow an' shcrape wid his fut, thin
they wint on together an' fell into discoorse.

"''T is a black night for thravelin',' says the Pooka.

"'Indade it is,' says the king, 'it's not me that 'ud be out
in it, if it was n't a case o' needcessity. I'm on an arriant av
charity,' says he.

"'That's rale good o' ye,' says the Pooka to him, 'and if
I may make bowld to ax, phat's the needcessity?'

"''T is to relave a widdy-woman,' says the king.

"'Oho,' says the Pooka, a-throwin' back his head laughin'
wid great plazin'ness an' nudgin' the king wid his leg on the
arrum, beways that it was a joke it was bekase the king said
it was to relave a widdy he was goin'. 'Oho,' says the Pooka,
''t is mesilf that's glad to be in the comp'ny av an iligint jin-
tleman that's on so plazin' an arriant av marcy,' says he.
'An' how owld is the widdy-woman?' says he, bustin' wid the
horrid laugh he had.

"'Musha thin,' says the king, gettin' red in the face an' not
likin' the joke the laste bit, for jist betune us, they do say
that afore he married the quane, he was the laddy-buck wid
the wimmin, an' the quane's maid towld the cook, that towld
the footman, that said to the gârdener, that towld the nabers
that many's the night the poor king was as wide awake as a
hare from sun to sun wid the quane a-gostherin' at him about

that same. More betoken, there was a widdy in it, that was
as sharp as a rat-thrap an' surrounded him whin he was young
an' had n't as much sinse as a goose, an' was like to marry
him at wanst in shpite av all his relations, as widdys undhershtand how to do. So it 's my consate that it was n't dacint
for the Pooka to be afther laughin' that-a-way, an' shows that

avil sper'ts is dirthy blaggârds that can't talk wid jintlemin.
'Musha,' thin, says the king, bekase the Pooka's laughin' was
n't agrayble to listen to, 'I don't know that same, fur I niver
seen her, but, be jagers, I belave she 's a hundherd, an' as ugly
as Belzebub, an' whin her owld man was alive, they tell me
she had a timper like a gandher, an' was as aisey to manage as

an armful o' cats,' says he. 'But she 's in want, an' I 'm afther bringin' her a suv'rin,' says he.

" Well, the Pooka sayced his laughin', fur he seen the king was very vexed, an' says to him, 'And if it 's plazin', where does she live ? '

" ' At the ind o' the boreen beyant the Corkschrew,' says the king, very short.

" ' Begob, that 's a good bit,' says the Pooka.

" ' Faix, it 's thrue for ye,' says the king, 'more betoken, it 's up hill ivery fut o' the way, an' me back is bruk entirely wid the stapeness,' says he, be way av a hint he 'd like a ride.

" ' Will yer Honor get upon me back,' says the Pooka. ' Sure I 'm afther goin' that-a-way, an' you don't mind gettin' a lift ? ' says he, a-fallin' like the stupid baste he was, into the thrap the king had made fur him.

" ' Thanks,' says the king, 'I b'lave not. I 've no bridle nor saddle,' says he, ' besides, it 's the shpring o' the year, an' I 'm afeared ye 're sheddin', an' yer hair 'ull come aff an' spile me new britches,' says he, lettin' on to make axcuse.

" ' Have no fear,' says the Pooka. ' Sure I niver drop me hair. It 's no ordhinary garron av a horse I am, but a most oncommon baste that 's used to the quolity,' says he.

" ' Yer spache shows that,' says the king, the clever man that he was, to be perlite that-a-way to a Pooka, that 's known to be a divil out-en-out, ' but ye must exqueeze me this avenin', bekase, d'ye mind, the road 's full o' shtones an' monsthrous stape, an' ye look so young, I 'm afeared ye 'll shtumble an' give me a fall,' says he.

" ' Arrah thin,' says the Pooka, ' it 's thrue fur yer Honor, I do look young,' an' he begun to prance on the road givin' himself airs like an owld widdy man afther wantin' a young woman, ' but me age is owlder than ye 'd suppoge. How owld 'ud ye say I was,' says he, shmilin'.

"IF IT 'S AGGRAYBLE TO YE, I 'LL LOOK IN YER MOUTH." Page 33.

" ' Begorra, divil a bit know I,' says the king, ' but if it's agrayble to ye, I 'll look in yer mouth an' give ye an answer,' says he.

" So the Pooka come up to him fair an' soft an' stratched his mouth like as he thought the king was wantin' fur to climb in, an' the king put his hand on his jaw like as he was goin' to see the teeth he had : and thin, that minnit he shlipped the three hairs round the Pooka's jaw, an' whin he done that, he dhrew thim tight, an' said the charm crossin' himself the while, an' immejitly the hairs wor cords av stale, an' held the Pooka tight, be way av a bridle.

" ' Arra-a-a-h, now, ye bloody baste av a murtherin' divil ye,' says the king, pullin' out his big whip that he had consaled in his top-coat, an' giving the Pooka a crack wid it undher his stummick, ' I 'll give ye a ride ye won't forgit in a hurry,' says he, ' ye black Turk av a four-legged nagur an' you shtaling me white mare,' says he, hittin' him agin.

" ' Oh my,' says the Pooka, as he felt the grip av the iron on his jaw an' knewn he was undher an inchantmint, ' Oh my, phat 's this at all,' rubbin' his breast wid his hind heel, where the whip had hit him, an' thin jumpin' wid his fore feet out to cotch the air an' thryin' fur to break away. ' Sure I 'm ruined, I am, so I am,' says he.

" ' It 's thrue fur ye,' says the king, ' begob it 's the wan thrue thing ye iver said,' says he, a-jumpin' on his back, an' givin' him the whip an' the two shpurs wid all his might.

" Now I forgot to tell ye that whin the king made his inchantmint, it was good fur siven miles round, and the Pooka knewn that same as well as the king an' so he shtarted like a cunshtable was afther him, but the king was afeared to let him go far, thinkin' he 'd do the siven miles in a jiffy, an' the inchantmint 'ud be broken like a rotten shtring, so he turned him up the Corkscrew.

"'I'll give ye all the axercise ye want,' says he, 'in thravellin' round this hill,' an' round an' round they wint, the king shtickin' the big shpurs in him every jump an' crackin' him wid the whip till his sides run blood in shtrames like a mill race, an' his schreams av pain wor heard all over the worruld so that the king av France opened his windy and axed the polisman why he did n't shtop the fightin' in the

shtrate. Round an' round an' about the Corkschrew wint the king, a-lashin' the Pooka, till his feet made the path ye see on the hill bekase he wint so often.

"And whin mornin' come, the Pooka axed the king phat he 'd let him go fur, an' the king was gettin' tired an' towld him that he must niver shtale another horse, an' never kill another man, barrin' furrin blaggârds that was n't Irish, an' whin he give a man a ride, he must bring him back to the shpot where he got him an' lave him there. So the Pooka consinted, Glory be to God, an' got aff, an' that 's the way he was tamed, an' axplains how it was that Dennis O'Rourke was left be the Pooka in the ditch jist where he found him."

" More betoken, the Pooka 's an althered baste every way, fur now he dhrops his hair like a common horse, and it 's often found shtickin' to the hedges where he jumped over, an' they do say he does n't shmell half as shtrong o' sulfur as he used, nor the fire out o' his nose is n't so bright. But all the king did fur him 'ud n't taiche him to be civil in his spache, an' whin he meets ye in the way, he spakes just as much like a blaggârd as ever. An' it 's out av divilmint entirely he does it, bekase he can be perlite as ye know be phat I towld ye av him sayin' to the king, an' that proves phat I said to ye that avil sper'ts can't larn rale good manners, no matther how hard they thry.

" But the fright he got never left him, an' so he kapes out av the highways an' thravels be the futpaths, an' so is n't often seen. An' it 's my belafe that he can do no harrum at all to thim that fears God, an' there 's thim that says he niver shows himself nor meddles wid man nor mortial barrin' they 're in dhrink, an' mebbe there 's something in that too, fur it does n't take much dhrink to make a man see a good dale."

THE SEXTON OF CASHEL.

ALL over Ireland, from Cork to Belfast, from Dublin to Galway, are scattered the ruins of churches, abbeys, and ecclesiastical buildings, the relics of a country once rich, prosperous and populous. These ruins raise their castellated walls and towers, noble even in decay, sometimes in the midst of a village, crowded with the miserably poor, sometimes on a mountain, in every direction commanding magnificent prospects; sometimes on an island in one of the lakes, which, like emeralds in a setting of deeper green, gem the surface of the rural landscape and contribute to increase the beauty of scenery not surpassed in the world.

Ages ago the voice of prayer and the song of praise ceased to ascend from these sacred edifices, and they are now visited only by strangers, guides, and parties of humble peasants, the foremost bearing on their shoulders the remains of a companion to be laid within the hallowed enclosure, for although the church is in ruins, the ground in and about it is still holy and in service when pious hands lay away in the bosom of earth the bodies of those who have borne the last burden, shed the last tear, and succumbed to the last enemy. But among all the pitiable spectacles presented in this un-

THE ROCK OF CASHEL. Page 40.

happy country, none is better calculated to inspire sad reflections than a rural graveyard. The walls of the ruined church tower on high, with massive cornice and pointed window; within stand monuments and tombs of the Irish great; kings, princes, and archbishops lie together, while about the hallowed edifice are huddled the graves of the poor; here, sinking so as to be indistinguishable from the sod; there, rising in new-made proportions; yonder, marked with a wooden cross, or a round stick, the branch of a tree rudely trimmed, but significant as the only token bitter poverty could furnish of undying love; while over all the graves, alike of the high born and of the lowly, the weeds and nettles grow.

"Sure there's no saxton, Sorr," said car-man Jerry Magwire, in answer to a question, "We dig the graves ourselves whin we put them away, an' sometimes there's a fight in the place whin two berryin's meet. Why is that? Faith, it's not for us to be talkin' o' them deep subjects widout respict, but it's the belafe that the last wan berrid must be carryin' wather all the time to the sowls in Purgathory till the next wan comes to take the place av him. So, ye mind, when two berryin's happen to meet, aitch party is shtrivin' to be done foorst, an' wan thries to make the other lave aff, an' thin they have it. Troth, Irishmen are too handy wid their fishts entirely, it's a weak pint wid 'em. But it's a sad sight, so it is, to see the graves wid the nettles on thim an' the walls all tumblin'. It is n't every owld church that has a caretaker like him of Cashel. Bedad, he was betther nor a flock av goats to banish the weeds.

"Who was he? Faith, I niver saw him but the wan time, an' thin I had only a shot at him as he was turnin' a corner, for it was as I was lavin' Cormac's chapel the time I wint to

Cashel on a pinance, bekase av a little throuble on me mind along av a pig that was n't mine, but got mixed wid mine whin I was afther killin' it. But, as I obsarved, it was only a shot at him I had, for it was n't aften that he was seen in the daytime, but done all his work in the night, an' it is n't me that 'ud be climbin' the Rock av Cashel afther the sun 'ud go to slape. Not that there 's avil sper'ts there, for none that 's bad can set fut on that holy ground day or night, but I 'm not afther wantin' to meet a sper't av any kind, even if it 's good, for how can ye tell about thim. Sure aven the blessed saints have been desaved, an' it 's not for a sinner like me to be settin' up for to know more than thimselves. But it was the long, bent body that he had, like he 'd a burdhen on his back, as they say, God be good to him, he had on his sowl, an' a thin, white face wid the hair an' beard hangin' about it, an' the great, blue eyes lookin' out as if he was gaz-in' on the other worruld. No, I did n't run down the rock, but I did n't walk aither, but jist bechuxt the two, wid a sharp eye round the corners that I passed. No more do I belave there was harrum in him, but, God's prisence be about us, ye can't tell.

"He was a man o' Clare be the name av Paddy O'Sullivan, an' lived on the highway betune Crusheen an' Ennis, an' they do say that whin he was a lad, there was n't a finer to be seen in the County; a tall, shtrappin' young felly wid an eye like a bay'net, an' a fisht like a shmith, an' the fut an' leg av him 'ud turn the hearts o' half the wimmin in the parish. An' they was all afther him, like they always do be whin a man is good lookin', sure I 've had a little o' that same ex-parience mesilf. Ye need n't shmile. I know me head has no more hair on it than an egg, an' I think me last tooth 'ull come out tomorrer, bad cess to the day, but they do say that

forty years ago, I cud have me pick av the gurruls, an' mebbe
they 're mishtaken an' mebbe not. But I was sayin', the
gurruls were afther Paddy like rats afther chaze, an' sorra a
wan o' thim but whin she spied him on the road, 'ud shlip behind the hedge to shmooth her locks a bit an' set the shawl
shtraight on her head. An' whin there was a bit av a dance,
niver a boy 'ud get a chance till Paddy made his chice to
dance wid, an' sorra a good word the rest o' the gurruls 'ud
give that same. Och, the tongues that wimmin have ! Sure
they 're sharper nor a draggin's tooth. Faith, I know that
well too, for I married two o' them an' larned a deal too
afther doin' it, an' axin' yer pardon, it 's my belafe that if
min knewn as much before marryin' as afther, bedad, the
owld maid population 'ud be greatly incrased.

"Howandiver, afther a bit, Paddy left carin' for thim all,
that, in my consate, is a moighty safe way, and begun to look
afther wan. Her name was Nora O'Moore, an' she was as
clever a gurrul as 'ud be found bechuxt Limerick an' Galway.
She was kind o' resarved like, wid a face as pale as a shroud,
an' hair as black as a crow, an' eyes that looked at ye an'
never seen ye. No more did she talk much, an' whin Paddy
'ud be sayin' his fine spaches, she 'd listen wid her eyes cast
down, an' whin she 'd had enough av his palaver, she 'd jist
look at him, an' somehow Paddy felt that his p'liteness was
n't the thing to work wid. He cud n't undhershtand her,
an' bedad, many 's the man that 's caught be not undhershtandin' thim. There 's rivers that 's quiet on top bekase
they 're deep, an' more that 's quiet bekase they 're not deep
enough to make a ripple, but phat 's the differ if ye can't
sound thim, an' whin a woman 's quiet, begorra, it 's not aisy
to say if she 's deep or shallow. But Nora was a deep wan,
an' as good as iver drew a breath. She thought a dale av

Paddy, only she 'd be torn limb from limb afore she 'd let
him know it till he confist first.   Well, my dear, Paddy wint
on, at firsht it was only purtindin' he was, an' whin he found
she cud n't be tuk wid his chaff, he got in airnest, an' afore
he knewn it, he was dead in love wid Nora, an' had as much
show for gettin' out agin as a shape in a bog, an' sorra a bit
did he know at all at all, whether she cared a traneen for
him.   It 's funny entirely that whin a man thinks a woman
is afther him, he 's aff like a hare, but if she does n't care a
rap, begob, he 'll give the nose aff his face to get her.   So it
was wid Paddy an' Nora, axceptin' that Paddy did n't know
that Nora wanted him as much as he wanted her.

  " So, wan night, whin he was bringin' her from a dance
that they 'd been at, he said to her that he loved her betther
than life an' towld her would she marry him, an' she axed
was it jokin' or in airnest he was, an' he said cud she doubt
it whin he loved her wid all the veins av his heart, an' she
trimbled, turnin' paler than iver, an' thin blushin' rosy red
for joy an' towld him yes, an' he kissed her, an' they both
thought the throuble was all over foriver.   It 's a way thim
lovers has, an' they must be axcused, bekase it 's the same
wid thim all.

  " But it was n't at all, fur Nora had an owld squireen av a
father, that was as full av maneness as eggs is av mate.   Sure
he was the divil entirely at home, an' niver left off wid the
crassness that was in him.   The timper av him was spiled be
rason o' losing his bit o' money wid cârds an' racin', an' like
some min, he tuk it out wid his wife an' dawther.   There was
only the three o' thim in it, an' they do say that whin he was
crazy wid dhrink, he 'd bate thim right an' lift, an' turn thim
out o' the cabin into the night, niver heeding, the baste, phat
'ud come to thim.   But they niver said a word thimselves, an'
the nabers only larned av it be seein' thim.

" Well. Whin O.'Moore was towld that Paddy was kapin'
comp'ny wid Nora, an' the latther an' her mother towld him
she wanted fur to marry Paddy, the owld felly got tarin' mad,
fur he was as proud as a paycock, an' though he 'd nothin'
himself, he riz agin the match, an' all the poor mother an'
Nora cud say 'ud n't sthir him.

" ' Sure I 've nothin' agin him,' he 'd say, ' barrin' he 's as
poor as a fiddler, an' I want Nora to make a good match.'

" Now the owld felly had a match in his mind fur Nora,
a lad from Tipperary, whose father was a farmer there, an'
had a shmart bit av land wid no end av shape grazin' on
it, an' the Tipperary boy was n't bad at all, only as shtupid as
a donkey, an' whin he 'd come to see Nora, bad cess to the

word he'd to say, only look at her a bit an' thin fall aslape an' knock his head agin the wall. But he wanted her, an' his father an' O'Moore put their heads together over a glass an' aggrade that the young wans 'ud be married.

"'Sure I don't love him a bit, father,' Nora 'ud say.

"'Be aff wid yer nonsinse,' he'd say to her. 'Phat does it matther about love, whin he's got more nor a hunderd shape. Sure I wud n't give the wool av thim fur all the love in Clare,' says he, an' wid that the argymint 'ud end.

"So Nora towld Paddy an' Paddy said he'd not give her up for all the men in Tipperary or all the shape in Ireland, an' it was aggrade that in wan way or another, they'd be married in spite av owld O'Moore, though Nora hated to do it, bekase, as I was afther tellin' ye, she was a good gurrul, an' wint to mass an' to her duty reg'lar. But like the angel that she was, she towld her mother an' the owld lady was agrayble, an' so Nora consinted.

"But O'Moore was shrewder than a fox whin he was sober, an' that was whin he'd no money to shpend in dhrink, an' this bein' wan o' thim times, he watched Nora an' begun to suspicion somethin'. So he made belave that everything was right an' the next time that Murphy, that bein' the name o' the Tipperary farmer, came, the two owld fellys settled it that O'Moore an' Nora 'ud come to Tipperary av the Winsday afther, that bein' the day o' the fair in Ennis that they knew Paddy 'ud be at, an' whin they got to Tipperary, they'd marry Nora an' young Murphy at wanst. So owld Murphy was to sind the câr afther thim an' everything was made sure. So, av the Winsday, towards noon, says owld O'Moore to Nora, —

"'Be in a hurry now, me child, an' make yersel' as fine as ye can, an' Murphy's câr 'ull be here to take us to the fair.'

" Nora did n't want to go, for Paddy was comin' out in the afthernoon, misthrustin' that owld O'Moore 'ud be at the fair. But O'Moore only towld her to make haste wid hersilf or they 'd be late, an' she did. So the câr came, wid a boy dhriving, an' owld O'Moore axed the boy if he wanted to go to the fair, so that Nora cud n't hear him, an' the boy said yes, an' O'Moore towld him to go an' he 'd dhrive an' bring him back tomorrer. So the boy wint away, an' O'Moore an' Nora got up an' shtarted. Whin they came to the crass-road, O'Moore tuk the road to Tipperary.

" ' Sure father, ye 're wrong,' says Nora, ' that 's not the way.'

" ' No more is it,' said the owld desayver, ' but I 'm afther wantin' to see a frind o' mine over here a bit an' we 'll come round to the Ennis road on the other side,' says he.

" So Nora thought no more av it, but whin they wint on an' on, widout shtoppin' at all, she begun to be disquisitive agin.

" ' Father, is it to Ennis or not ye 're takin' me,' says she.

" Now, be this time, they 'd got on a good bit, an' the owld villin seen it was no use thryin' to desave her any longer.

" ' I 'm not,' says he, ' but it 's to Tipperary ye 're goin', where ye 're to be married to Misther Murphy this blessed day, so ye are, an' make no throuble about it aither, or it 'll be the worse for ye,' says he, lookin' moighty black.

" Well, at first Nora thought her heart 'ud shtand still. ' Sure, Father dear, ye don't mane it, ye cud n't be so cruel. It 's like a blighted tree I 'd be, wid that man,' an' she thried to jump aff the câr, but her father held her wid a grip av stale.

" ' Kape still,' says he wid his teeth closed like a vise. ' If

ye crass me, I'm like to murdher ye. It's me only escape
from prison, for I'm in debt an' Murphy 'ull help me,' says
he. 'Sure,' says he, saftenin' a bit as he seen the white face
an' great pleadin' eyes, 'Sure ye'll be happy enough wid
Murphy. He loves ye, an' ye can love him, an' besides, think
o' the shape.'

"But Nora sat there, a poor dumb thing, wid her eyes
lookin' deeper than iver wid the misery that was in thim.
An' from that minit, she did n't spake a word, but all her
sowl was detarmined that she'd die afore she'd marry Murphy, but how she'd get out av it she did n't know at all, but
watched her chance to run.

"Now it happened that owld O'Moore, bein' disturbed in
his mind, mistuk the way, an' whin he come to the crass-roads,
wan to Tipperary an' wan to Cashel, he tuk the wan for the
other, an' whin the horse thried to go home to Tipperary, he
wud n't let him, but pulled him into the Cashel road. Faix, he
might have knewn that if he'd let the baste alone, he'd take
him right, fur horses knows a dale more than ye'd think.
That horse o' mine is only a common garron av a baste, but
he tuk me from Ballyvaughn to Lisdoon Varna wan night
whin it was so dark that ye cud n't find yer nose, an' wint be
the rath in a gallop, like he'd seen the good people. But
niver mind, I'll tell ye the shtory some time, only I was
thinkin' O'Moore might have knewn betther.

"But they tuk the Cashel road an' wint on as fast as they
cud, for it was afthernoon an' gettin' late. An' O'Moore kept
lookin' about an' wonderin' that he did n't know the counthry, though he'd niver been to Tipperary but wanst, an'
afther a while, he gev up that he was lost entirely. No more
wud he ax the people on the road, but gev thim 'God save
ye' very short, for he was afeared Nora might make throuble.

An' by an' by, it come on to rain, an' whin they turned the corner av a hill, he seen the Rock o' Cashel wid the churches on it, an' thin he stopped.

" ' Phat 's this at all,' says he. ' Faix, if that is n't Cashel I 'll ate it, an' we 've come out o' the way altogether.'

" Nora answered him niver a word, an' he shtarted to turn round, but whin he looked at the horse, the poor baste was knocked up entirely.

" ' We 'll go on to Cashel,' says he, ' an' find a shebeen, an' go back in the mornin'. It 's hard luck we 're afther havin',' says he.

" So they wint on, an' jist afore they got to the Rock, they seen a nate lodgin' house be the road an' wint in. He left Nora to sit be the fire, while he wint to feed the horse, an' whin he come back in a minit, he looked for her, but faith, she 'd given him the shlip an' was gone complately.

" ' Where is me daw-ther ? ' says he.

" ' Faith, I dunno,' says the maid. ' She walked out av the dure on the minit,' says she.

" Owld O'Moore run, an' Satan an' none but himself turned him in the way she was afther takin.' God be good to thim, no wan iver knewn phat tuk place, but whin they wint wid a lanthern to sarch

fur thim whin they did n't raturn, they found the marks o'
their feet on the road to the strame. Half way down the
path they picked up Nora's shawl that was torn an' flung
on the ground an' fut marks in plenty they found, as if he
had caught her an' thried to howld her an' cud n't, an' on
the marks wint to the high bank av the strame, that was a
torrent be razon av the rain. An' there they ended wid a big
slice o' the bank fallen in, an' the sarchers crassed thimselves
wid fright an' wint back an' prayed for the repose av their
sowls.

"The next day they found thim, a good Irish mile down
the strame, owld O'Moore wid wan hand howlding her gown
an' the other wan grippin' her collar an' the clothes half torn
aff her poor cowld corpse, her hands stratched out afore her,
wid the desperation in her heart to get away, an' her white
face wid the great eyes an' the light gone out av thim, the
poor craythur, God give her rest, an' so to us all.

"They laid thim dacintly, wid candles an' all, an' the wake
that they had was shuparb, fur the shtory was towld in all
the counthry, wid the vartues av Nora; an' the O'Brian's
come from Ennis, an' the O'Moore's from Crusheen, an' the
Murphy's an' their frinds from Tipperary, an' more from
Clonmel. There was a power av atin' an' slathers av dhrink
fur thim that wanted it, fur, d' ye mind, thim of Cashel
thried fur to show the rale Irish hoshpitality, bekase O'Moore
an' Nora were sint there to die an' they thought it was their
juty to thrate thim well. An' all the County Clare an' Tipperary was at the berryin', an' they had three keeners, the
best that iver was, wan from Ennis, wan from Tipperary, an'
wan from Limerick, so that the praises av Nora wint on day
an' night till the berryin' was done. An' they made Nora's
grave in Cormac's Chapel just in front o' the Archbishop's

tomb in the wall an' berried her first, an' tuk O'Moore as far from her as they cud get him, an' put his grave as clost be the wall as they cud go fur the shtones an' jist ferninst the big gate on the left hand side, an' berried him last, an' sorra the good word they had fur him aither.

"Poor Paddy wint nayther to the wake nor to the berryin', fur afther they towld him the news, he sat as wan in a dhrame, no more cud they rouse him. He 'd go to his work very quite, an' niver shpake a word. An' so it was, about a fortnight afther, he says to his mother, says he, 'Mother I seen Nora last night an' she stood be me side an' laid her hand on me brow, an' says "Come to Cashel, Paddy dear, an' be wid me." ' An' his mother was frighted entirely, for she parsaved he was wrong in his head. She thried to aise his mind, but the next night he disappared. They folly 'd him to Cashel, but he dodged an' kept from thim complately whin they come an' so they left him. In the day he 'd hide an' slape, an' afther night, Nora's sper't 'ud mate him an' walk wid him up an' down the shtones av the Chapel an' undher the arches av the Cathaydral, an' he cared fur her grave, an' bekase she was berried there, fur the graves av all thim that shlept on the Rock. No more had he any frinds, but thim o' Cashel 'ud lave pitaties an' bread where he 'd see it an' so he lived. Fur sixty wan years was he on the Rock an' never left it, but he 'd sometimes show himself in the day whin there was a berryin', an' say, 'Ye 've brought me another frind,' an' help in the work, an' never was there a graveyard kept like that o' Cashel.

"When he got owld, an' where he cud look into the other worruld, Nora came ivery night an' brought more wid her, sper'ts av kings an' bishops that rest on Cashel, an' there 's thim that 's seen the owld man walkin' in Cormac's Chapel,

Nora holdin' him up an' him discoorsin' wid the mighty dead. They found him wan day, cowld an' shtill, on Nora's grave, an' laid him be her side, God rest his sowl, an' there he slapes to-day, God be good to him.

"They said he was only a poor owld innocent, but all is aqualized, an' thim that's despised sometimes have betther comp'ny among the angels than that of mortials."

SATAN'S CLOVEN HOOF.

AMONG the beautiful traits of the Irish character, none is more prominent than the religious element. Philosophers declare that the worshipping principle is strong in proportion to the lack of happiness in the circumstances of life, and at first glance there seems a degree of truth in the statement; for the rich, enjoying their riches, are likely to be contented and to look no further than this world; while the poor, oppressed and ground to the earth by those whom they feel to be no better than themselves, having that innate sense of justice common to all men, and discerning the inequality of worldly lots, are not slow to place implicit belief in the doctrine of a final judgment, at which all inequalities will be righted, and both rich and poor will stand side by side; the former gaining no advantage from his riches, the latter being at no disadvantage from his poverty.

There is, however, good reason to believe that in the days of Ireland's greatness there was the same strength of devotion as at present. Ireland is so full of ruined churches and ecclesiastical buildings as to give color of truth to the statement of a recent traveller, " it is a country of ruins." Rarely is the traveller out of sight of the still standing walls of a long deserted church, and not infrequently the churches are found in groups. The barony of Forth, in Wexford, though comprising a territory of only 40,000 acres, contains the ruins of eighteen churches, thirty-three chapels, two convents, and a hospital of vast proportions. Nor is this district exceptional, for at Glendalough, Clon-mac-nois, Inniscathy, Inch Derrin, and Innis Kealtra, there are groups of churches, each group having seven churches, the edifices of goodly size, and at Clonferth and Holy Cross, there are seven chapels in each town, so close together as to cause wonder whether all were called into use.

One manifestation of the religious element of the Irish nature is seen in the profound reverence for the memory of the saints. Of these, Ireland claims, according to one authority, no less than seventy-five thousand, and it is safe to say that the curious inquirer might find one or more legends of each, treasured up in the unwritten folk-lore of the country districts. To the disadvantage of the minor saints, however, most of the stories cluster round a few well-known names, and nothing delights the Irish story-teller more than to relate legends of the saints, which he does with a particularity as minute in all its details as though he had stood by the side of the saint, had seen everything that was done, and heard every word that was spoken; supplying missing links in the chain of the story from a ready imagination, and throwing over the whole the glamour of poetic fancy inseparable from the Irish nature.

The neighborhood of Glendalough, County Wicklow, is sacred to the memory of Saint Kevin, and abounds with legends of his life and works. The seven churches which, according to tradition, were built there under his direction, are now mostly in ruins; his bed, a hollow in a precipice, is still shown, together with his kitchen and the altar at which he once ministered. In the graveyard of one of the churches is a curious stone cross, of considerable size, evidently monumental, though the inscription has been so defaced as to be illegible. On the front of the cross there is a deep indentation much resembling that made by the hoof of a cow in soft earth, the bottom of the indentation being deepest at the sides and somewhat ridged in the middle. Concerning this cross and the de-

pression in its face, the following legend was related by an old peasant of the neighborhood.

"Ye must know, that among all the saints that went to heaven from Ireland's sod, there is n't wan, barrin' Saint Patrick, that stands in a betther place than the blessed Saint Kevin av Glendalough, fur the wondherful things that he done is past all tellin'. 'T was he that built all the churches ye see

in the vale here, an' when he lived, he owned all the land
round about, fur he restored King O'Toole's goose, that the
king had such divarshun in, when it was too ould to fly, so
the king gev him all that the goose 'ud fly over, an' when the
goose got her wings agin, she was so merry that she flew over
mighty near all the land that King O'Toole had before she
come back at all, so he got it.

"'T was he too that put out o' the counthry the very last
sarpint that was left in it, afther Saint Patrick had druv the
rest into the say, fur he met the baste wan day as he was walkin' in the hills and tuk him home wid him to give him the bit
an' sup, an' the sarpint got as dhrunk as a piper, so Saint
Kevin put him in a box an' nailed it up an' flung it into the
say, where it is to this blessed day.

"But 't is my belafe that the besht job o' work he ever
done was markin' the divil so if you 'd meet him an the road,
you 'd know in a minnit that it was himself an' no other that
was in it, an' so make ready, aither fur to run away from him,
or to fight him wid prayin' as fast as ye cud, bekase, ye see,
it 's no use fur to shtrive wid him any other way, seein' that
no waypon can make the laste dint on his carkidge.

"In thim days, an' before phat tuk place I 'm tellin' ye av,
the divil was all as wan as a man, a tall felly like a soger, wid
a high hat comin' to a pint an' feathers on it, an' fine boots
an' shpurs an' a short red jacket wid a cloak over his shoulder
an' a soord be his side, as fine as any gintleman av' the good
ould times. So he used to go about the counthry, desavin'
men an' wimmin, the latther bein' his chice as bein' aisier fur
to desave, an' takin' thim down wid him to his own place, an'
it was a fine time he was havin' entirely, an' everything his
own way. Well, as he was thravellin' about, he heard wan
day av Saint Kevin an' the church he was afther buildin' an'

the haythens he was convartin' an' he says to himself, ' Sure this won't do. I must give up thriflin' an' look afther me bizness, or me affairs 'ull go to the dogs, so they will.'

" It was in Kerry he was when he heard the news, an' was havin' a fine time there, fur when Saint Patrick convarted Ireland, he did n't go to Kerry, but only looked into it an' blessed it an' hurried on, but though he did n't forget it, intindin', I belave, to go back, the divil tuk up his quarthers there, to make it as sure as he cud. But when he heard av Saint Kevin's doin's, it was too much fur him, so he shtarted an' come from Kerry to Glendalough wid wan jump, an' there sure enough, the walls o' the church were risin' afore his eyes, an' as he stud on that hill he heard the avenin' song o' the monks that were helpin' Saint Kevin in the work. So the divil was tarin' mad, an' stud on the brow o' the hill, cursin' to himself an' thinkin' that if any more churches got into Ireland, his job o' work 'ud be gone, an' he 'd betther go back to England where he come from. He made up his mind though, that he 'd do fur Saint Kevin if he cud, but mind ye, the blessed saint was so well beknownst to all the counthry, that the divil was afeared to tackle him. So he laid about in the grass, on his breast like a sarpint fur three or four days till they were beginnin' to put the roof on, and then he thought he 'd thry.

" Now I must tell ye wan thing. The blessed saint was at that time only a young felly, though they don't make 'em any betther than he was. When he left home, he 'd a shweetheart be the name o' Kathleen, an' she loved him betther than her life, an' so did he her in that degray that he 'd lay down an' die on the shpot fur the love av her, but his juty called him fur to be God's priest, an' he turned his back on father an' mother an' saddest av all on Kathleen, though it was like tarin' out his heart it was, an' came to Glendalough. Kathleen was like to die, but afther a bit, she got over it a little an' went into a convent, for, says she, ' I 'll marry no wan, an' 'ull meet him in heaven.' But Saint Kevin did n't know phat had become av her, an' thried hard not to think av her, but wanst in a while the vision av her 'ud come back to him like the mem'ry av a beautiful dhrame.

" Now about this time, while the divil was layin' about in the bushes a-watchin' the work, an' the tower of the big church was liftin' itself above the trees, the blessed saint begun to be onaisy in his mind, fur, says he to himself, ' Things is too aisy entirely. It 's just thim times when all is goin' on as smooth as a duck on a pond that the divil comes down like a fox on a goslin' an' takes every wan unbeknownst, so wins the vict'ry. I 'll have a care, fur afther the sunshine comes the shtorm,' says he. So that avenin' he ordhered his monks to say a thousand craydos, an' two thousand paters an' aves, an' afther that was done, he got in his boat an' crassed the lake. He climbed up to his bed above ye there, an' said his baids agin an' went to slape, but the divil was watchin' him like a hawk, for he 'd laid a thrap fur the blessed saint to catch him wid, that was thish-a-way.

" Every body knows how that Satan is shlicker than a weasel, an' has a mem'ry like a miser's box that takes in everything an' lets nothin' go out. When ye do anything, sorra a bit av it 'scapes the divil, an' he hugs it clost till a time comes when he can make a club av it to bate ye wid, an' so he does. The owld felly remimbered all that passed betune Kathleen an' the blessed saint, an' he knewn how hard it was fur Saint Kevin to forgit her, so he thought he 'd put him in a fix. Afther the saint had cuddled up in his shtraw wid his cloak over him an' was shnoring away as snug as a flea in a blanket, comes the divil, a-climbin' up the rock, in the exact image o' the young Kathleen. Ye may think it quare, but it's no wondher to thim that undherstands it, fur the divil can take any shape he plazes an' look like any wan he wants to, an' so he does for the purpose av temptin' us poor sinners to disthruction, but there's wan thing be which he's always known; when ye 've given up to him or when ye 've baten him out o' the face, no matther which, he 's got to throw aff the disguise that's on him an' show you who he is, an' when he does it, it is n't the iligant, dressed-up divil that ye see an' that I was just tellin' ye av, but the rale, owld, black nagur av a rannychorus, widout a haporth o' rags to the back av him, an' his horns an' tail a-shtickin' out, an' his eyes as big as an oxen's an' shinin' like fire, an' great bat's wings on him, an', savin' yer prisince, the most nefairius shmell o' sulfur ye ever shmelt. But before, he looks all right, no matther phat face he has, an' it 's only be the goodness o' God that the divil is bound fur to show himself to ye, bekase, Glory be to God, it 's his will that men shall know who they 're dalin' wid, an' if they give up to the divil, an' afther findin' out who 's in it, go on wid the bargain they 've made, sure the fault is their own, an' they go to hell wid their eyes open, an' if they bate him, he 's got to show himself fur to let thim see phat they 've escaped.

"Well, I was afther sayin', the divil was climbin' up the rock in the form o' Kathleen, an' come to the saint's bed an' teched him an the shouldher. The blessed saint was layin' there belike dhraming o' Kathleen, fur sure, there was no harm in that, an' when he woke up an' seen her settin' be his side, he thought the eyes 'ud lave him.

"'Kathleen,' says he, 'is it yoursilf that 's in it, an' me thinkin' I 'd parted from you forever?'

"'It is,' says the ould desaver, 'an' no other, Kevin darlint, an' I 've come to shtay wid ye.'

" ' Sure darlint,' says the saint, ' ye know how it bruk me heart entirely to lave ye, no more wud I have done it, but be the will o' God. Ye know I loved ye, an' God forgive me, I 'm afeared I love ye still, but it is n't right, Kathleen. Go in pace, in the name o' God, an' lave me,' says he.

" ' No Kevin,' says Satan, a-throwin' himself on Kevin's breast, wid both arrums round his neck, ' I 'll never lave ye,' lettin' an to cry an' dhrop tears an the face o' the blessed saint.

" It 's no aisy matther to say no to a woman anyhow, aven to an ugly woman, but when it 's a good-lookin' wan that 's in it, an' she axin' ye wid her arrums round ye an' the crystal dhrops like that many dimunds fallin' from her eyes that look at ye like shtars through a shower av rain, begob it 's meself that does n't undhershtand why Saint Kevin did n't give up at wanst, an' so he wud if he had n't been the blessed saint that he was. But he was mightily flusthered, an' no wondher, an' stud there wid his breast hayvin', a-shtrivin' to resist the timptation to thrade a crown in heaven fur a love on airth.

" ' Lave this place, Kevin,' says the tempther, ' an' come wid me, we 'll go away an' be happy together forever,' an' wid that word, an' as the fate av the saint was trimblin' in the balances, the holy angels o' God stud beside him, an' wan whishpered in his ear that the Kathleen he loved before was a pure, good woman, an' that she 'd 'a' died afore she 'd come to him that-a-way.

" ' No,' says he, wid sudden shtrength. ' It 's not Kathleen that 's in it, but an avil sper't. God's prisence be about us ! Get you gone Satan an' sayce to throuble me,' an' that minnit the blessed saint jumped up aff the ground an' wid his two feet gev the owld rayprobate a thunderin' kick in the stummick, an' when he doubled up wid the pain an' fell back an' clapped his hands together on the front av him, Saint Kevin gev him another in his rare, axin' yer pardon, that sent him clane over the clift, wid Saint Kevin gatherin' shtones an' flingin' thim afther him wid all the might that was in him. So the minnit the saint kicked him the very foorst kick, Kathleen disappeared, an' there was the owld black Belzebub a-tumblin' over, an' fallin' down to the lake, holdin' his stummick an' thryin' hard to catch himself wid his wings afore he 'd hit the wather. But he did by the time he got to the bottom an' flew away, bellerin' worse nor a bull with a dog hangin' to his nose, so that all the monks woke wid fright, an' cud n't go to shlape agin till they 'd said a craydo an' five aves apiece, but the blessed saint set be his bed a-sayin' his baids the rest o' the night wid a pile o' shtones convaynient to his hand fur fear the divil 'ud come back. But Satan flew over an that hill an' rubbed himself before an' behind too, where the saint had kicked him, an' did n't go back, for he 'd enough o' the saint fur that time. But he was mightily vexed, an' not to lose the chance fur to do some mischief before he 'd go away, he pulled down all the walls that the poor monks had built that day.

"Now there 's thim that says that it was the rale Kathleen that Saint Kevin kicked over the clift, but sure that 's not thrue, fur it 's not in an Irishman to thrate a woman that-a-way, that makes me belave that the shtory I 'm tellin' ye was the thrue shtory an' that it was n't Kathleen at all, but Satan, that Saint Kevin thrated wid such onpoliteness, an' my blessin' an him fur that same, fur he come out very well axceptin' five or six blisthers on his face, where the divil's tears touched him, that 's well known to make blisthers on phatever they touch.

"Well, as I was sayin', he pulled down the church walls,

an' the monks put thim up agin, an' the next mornin' they were down, an' so fur a good bit the contist went an betune the divil an' the monks, a-shtrivin' if they cud build up fashter than he cud pull down, fur he says to himself, Satan did, ‘Jagers, I can't be losin' me time here widout doin' something, nor, bedad, no more can I tell how to rache the saint widout sarcumspectin' him.’

“ But the saint bate him at that game, for wan night, afther the work was done, he put half the monks on the wall to watch there the night, an' when Satan come flyin' along like the dirthy bat that he was, there was the monks all along be the day's job, aitch wan a-sayin' his baids as fast as he cud an' a bottle o' holy wather be his side to throw at the divil when he 'd come. So he went from thim an' be takin' turns at watchin' an' workin', they finished the church.

“ In coorse o' time, Saint Kevin wanted another church an'

begun to build it too, for he said, 'Begob, I 'll have that church done be fall if every grain o' sand in Glendalough becomes a divil an' rises up fur to purvint it,' an' so he did, Glory be to God, but at first was bothered to git the money fur to raise the walls. Well, wan day as he was in the bother, he was walkin' an the hills, an' he heard the clattherin' av a horse's feet behind him an the road, an' afore he cud turn round, up comes the most illigant black horse ye ever seen, an' a tall gintleman a ridin' av him, wid all the look av a soger, a broad hat on the head av him, an' a silk jacket wid goold trimmin's, an' shtripes on his britches, an' gloves to his elbows, an' soord an' shpurs a-jinglin', the same as he was a rich lord.

" ' God save ye,' says the saint.

" ' God save ye kindly,' says the gintleman, an' they walked an together an' fell into convarsin'.

" ' I 'm towld ye 're afther buildin' another church,' says the gintleman.

" ' It 's thrue for ye,' says the saint, ' but it 's meself that 's bothered about that same, for I 've no money,' says he.

" ' That 's too bad,' says the gintleman ; ' have ye axed for help ? ' says he.

" ' Faix, indade I have,' says the saint, ' but the times is hard, an' the money goin' out o' the counthry to thim blaggârd landlords in England,' says he.

" ' It 's right ye are,' says the gintleman, ' but I 've hopes o' betther times when the tinants get the land in their own hands,' says he. ' I 'm goin' to right thim avils. I 'm the new Lord Liftinant,' says he, ' an' able to help ye an the job, undher a proper undhershtandin',' says he.

" At foorst Saint Kevin was that surprised that he 'd like to dhrop an the road, fur he had n't heard av the 'pintmint av a new Lord Liftinant, but he raizoned wid himself that it cud aisily be done widout his knowin' av it, an' so he thought he 'd a shtrake av luck in seein' av him.

" ' God be good to yer Lordship,' says he, ' an' make yer bed in the heavens, an' it 's thankful I 'd be fur any shmall favors ye plaze to give, fur it 's very poor we are.'

" ' An' phat 'ud ye say to a prisint av tin thousand pound,' says the gintleman, ' purvided ye spind it an the church ye have an' not in buildin' a new wan,' says the gintleman, an' wid that word, Saint Kevin knew the ould inimy, an' shtarted at him.

" But the divil had enough o' Saint Kevin's heels, for he 'd felt the kick he cud give wid 'em, an' faix, the blessed saint was as well sarcumstanced in that quarther as a donkey, an' Belzebub knew that same, so he niver stayed, but when he saw Saint Kevin comin', immejitly the black horse changed into a big dhraggin, an' the illigant close dhrapped aff the divil an' in his own image he went aff shpurrin' the dhraggin, he an' the baste flappin' their wings as fast as they cud to get out of the saint's way an' lavin' afther thim the shmell av sulfur that shtrong that the blessed saint did nothin' for an hour but hould his nose an' cough.

" Afther thim two axpayriences, the divil seen it was no use o' him offerin' fur to conthraven Saint Kevin, so he rayjuiced his efforts to botherin' the monks at the work. He 'd hang about day an' night, doin' all the mischief that he cud, bekase, says he, ' If I can't shtop thim, by Jayminy, I 'll delay thim to that degray that they 'll find it the shlowest job they ever undhertuk,' says he, an' so it was. When they 'd finish a bit o' the wall an' lave it to dhry, up 'ud come the divil an' kick it over; when two o' them 'ud be carrying a heavy shtone, the divil, unbeknownst to thim, 'ud knock it out o' their hands so as to make it dhrop on their toes, a-thinkin' belike, that they'd shwear on the quiet to thimselves: that they never did; when a holy father 'ud lay down his hammer an' turn his back, the divil 'ud snatch it up an' fling it aff the wall; till wid his knockin' over the wather-bucket, an' shcrapin' aff the mor-thar, an' upsettin' the hod o' bricks, an' makin' the monks forgit where they'd put things, it got so that they were in a muck o' shweat every hour o' the day; an' from that time it got to be said, when anything wint wrong widout a raizon, that the divil's in it.

"Now whin Saint Kevin conshecrated the church, they tuk wid it the ground round about as far as ye see that shtone wall, for, says he, 'Sure it'll always be handy.' So in coorse o' time, as the second church was gettin' done, wan avenin' Saint Kevin went out wid a bucket fur to milk his cow, that had just come down from the mountain where she'd been grazin'. Well, he let the calf to her, an' the poor little baste bein' hungry, fur I belave the cow had n't come up the night afore, it begun on wan side an' the saint an the other, an' the calf was suckin' away wid all the jaws it had, an' kep' up a haythenish punchin' wid its nose beways av a hint to the cow fur to give up more milk. The calf punched an' the cow kicked, fur, mind ye, the divil was in thim both, the poor bastes, no more was it their fault at all, an' betune howldin' the bucket in wan hand an' milking wid the other wan, an' kapin' his eye shkinned for the cow's heels, an' shovin' the calf from his side, the saint was like to lose all the milk.

"'Tatther an' agers,' says he, 'shtand shtill, ye onnatthe-ral crayther, or I'll bate the life out o' ye, so I will,' says he, tarin' mad, fur the calf was gettin' all, an' the bottom o' the bucket not covered. But the cow wud n't do it, so the blessed saint tuk the calf be the years fur to drag him away, an' then the cow run at him wid her horns so that he had to let go the calf's years an' dodge an' was in a bother entirely. But he got him a club in case the cow 'ud offer fur to hook him agin, an' opened the gate into the field behind the church, an' afther a good dale o' jumpin' about he sucsayded in dhrivin' in the cow an' kapin' out the calf. Then he shut the gate an' wipin' the shweat aff his blessed face, he got the bucket an' shtool an' set down to milk in pace. But be this time the cow was tarin' mad at bein' shut from the calf, an' at the first shquaze he gev her, she jumped like she 'd heard a banshee, an' then phat 'ud she do but lift up her heel an' give him a kick an the skull fit to crack it fur him an' laid him on the grass, an' turnin' round, she put her fut in the bucket an' stud lookin' at him, as fur to ax if he 'd enough.

" ' The divil brile the cow,' says the saint, God forgive him fur cursin' her, but ye see he 'd lost all consate av her be the throuble he 'd had wid her afore, besides the crack on his head, that was well nigh aiquel to the kick he cud give himself, so that he was axcusable fur phat he was sayin', fur it 's no joke I 'm tellin' ye to be made a showbogher av, be a baste av a cow.

" ' Sure I will, yer Riverince,' says a deep voice behind him, ' an' thank ye fur that same favor, fur it 's a fat bit she is.'

" Saint Kevin riz up a-rubbin' his head as fast as he cud an' looked round an' there sure enough was owld Satan himself standin' there grinnin' away wid the horrid mouth av him stratched from year to year, a-laughin' at the fix the saint was in. Well, the minnit Saint Kevin set his two eyes an him, he knewn he had him, fur ye see, the ground was conshecrated, but the divil did n't know it fur it was done wan time when he 'd gone to Cork to attind a landlord's convintion to raise the rints on a lot o' shtarving tinants, that bein' a favorite job wid him. If he 'd knewn the ground was holy, he 'd never dared to set fut an it, fur ye see, if ye can ketch the divil an holy ground where he 's no bizness, ye 've got him fast an' tight an' can pull him in when ye plaze. But the saint was n't goin' to give the owld desaver any show so he run at him an' gripped him be the horns, the same as he was a goat, an' threw him an the ground an' tied his hands wid a pace av his own gown that he tore aff, an' the divil, do phat he cud, was n't able to break loose.

" ' Now,' says he, ' ye slatherin', blood-suckin', blaggârdin' nagur, I 'll fix ye, ye owld hippypotaymus, so as ivery sowl in Ireland 'ull know ye where ever ye 're met.'

" So he rowled up his shlaves an' shpit an his hands an' fell to work. He onschrewed the divil's left leg at the jint av the knee, an' laid it an the grass. Then he tuk aff the cow's right hind leg at the knee an' laid that an the grass. Then he schrewed the owld cow's leg an the divil's knee, an' the divil's fut an the owld cow's leg, an' untied Satan an' bid him git up.

" ' Now,' says he to him, ' do you go at wanst, an' I bid ye that when ye meet man or mortial, the foorst thing ye do is to show that fut that they know from the shtart who ye are. Now shtart, ye vagabone blaggârd av a shpalpeen, or I 'll kick the backbone shtrait up into the shkull o' ye. Out!' he says, flourishin' his fut at him.

" Well, the divil made a break fur to run, bekase he wanted no more benedictions from the toes o' Saint Kevin, but not bein' used to his new leg, the very foorst shtep he made wid it, it kicked out behind agin this shtone, that was n't a crass at all then, an' made this hole that ye see, an' Saint Kevin tuk the shtone an' made a crass av it aftherwards. But the divil did n't shtop at all when the leg wud n't go fur him, fur he seen the blessed saint comin', a-wavin' his fut about, so he rowled over an' over till he got to the wall, then made a shpring an it an' out av sight like a ghost.

"That's the way Satan got his lame leg, bekase, ye see, he's niver larned fur to manage it, an' goes limpity-lop, an' though he wears a cloak, is obligated fur to show the cow's fut whenever he talks wid any wan, fur if he does n't, begorra, the leg does fur itself, fur it's niver forgot the thrick av kick-

ing the owld cow larned it, an' if Satan waits a minnit, up goes the cow's fut, as hard an' high as the last time she kicked the saint. No more did the divil ever dare to come there agin, so the blessed Saint Kevin was left in pace to build the siven churches, an the divil was n't ever seen in Glen- dalough, till the day the saint was ber- rid, an' then he peeped over the hill to look at the berryin', but he wud n't come down, thinkin', belike, it was a lie they were tellin' him when they said the saint was dead, fur to injuice him to come into the glen an' give Saint Kevin wan more whack at him wid his fut. An' they do say, that he's been to the besht docthers in the univaarse fur to get him another leg, but they cud n't do it, Glory be to God; an' so he is lame an' must show his cloven fut, so as ivery wan knows at wanst that it's the divil himself that's in it, an' can run away from him before he's time to do thim harm.

THE ENCHANTED ISLAND.

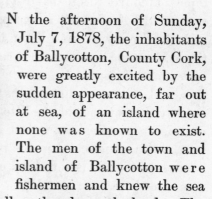 N the afternoon of Sunday, July 7, 1878, the inhabitants of Ballycotton, County Cork, were greatly excited by the sudden appearance, far out at sea, of an island where none was known to exist. The men of the town and island of Ballycotton were fishermen and knew the sea as well as they knew the land. The day before, they had been out in their boats and sailed over the spot where the strange island now appeared, and were certain that the locality was the best fishing-ground they had.

"And still they gazed, and still the wonder grew," for the day was clear and the island could be seen as plainly as they saw the hills to the north. It was rugged, in some parts rocky, in others densely wooded; here and there were deep shadows in its sides indicating glens heavily covered with undergrowth and grasses. At one end it rose almost precipitously from the sea; at the other, the declivity was gradual; the thick forest of the mountainous portion gave way to smaller trees, these to shrubs; these to green meadows that finally melted into the sea and became indistinguishable from the waves.

Under sail and oar, a hundred boats put off from the shore to investigate; when, as they neared the spot, the strange island became dim in outline, less vivid in color, and at last vanished entirely, leaving the wonder-stricken villagers to return, fully convinced that for the first time in their lives they had really seen the Enchanted Island. For once there was a topic of conversation that would outlast the day, and as the story of the Enchanted Island passed from lip to lip, both story and island grew in size till the latter was little less than a continent, containing cities and castles, palaces and cathedrals, towers and steeples, stupendous mountain ranges, fertile valleys, and wide spreading plains; while the former was limited only by the patience of the listener, and embraced the personal experience, conclusions, reflections, and observations of every man, woman, and child in the parish who had been fortunate enough to see the island, hear of it, or tell where it had been seen elsewhere.

For the Enchanted Island of the west coast is not one of those ordinary, humdrum islands that rise out of the sea in a night, and then, having come, settle down to business on scientific principles, and devote their attention to the collection of soil for the use of plants and animals. It disdains any such commonplace course as other islands are content to follow, but is peripatetic, or, more properly, seafaring, in its habits, and as fond of travelling as a sailor. At its own sweet will it comes, and, having shown itself long enough to convince everybody who is not an "innocent entirely" of its reality, it goes without leave-taking or ceremony, and always before boats can approach near enough to make a careful inspection. This is the invariable history of its appearance. No one has ever been able to come close to its shores, much less land upon them, but it has been so often seen on the west coast, that a doubt of its existence, if expressed in the company of coast fishermen, will at once establish for the sceptic a reputation for ignorance of the common affairs of every-day life.

In Cork, for instance, it has been seen by hundreds of people off Ballydonegan Bay, while many more can testify to its appearance off the Bay of Courtmacsherry. In Kerry, all the population of Ballyheige saw it a few years ago, lying in Tralee Bay, between Kerry Head and Brandon's Head, and shortly before, the villagers of Lisneakeabree, just across the bay from Ballyheige, saw it between their shore and Kerry Head, while the fishermen in Saint Finan's Bay and in Ballinskelligs are confident it has been seen, if not by themselves, at least by some of their friends. It has appeared at the mouth of the Shannon, and off Carrigaholt in Clare, where the people saw a city on it. This is not so remarkable as it seems, for, in justice to the Enchanted Island, it should be stated that its resemblance to portions of the neighboring land is sometimes very close, and shows that the " enchanter " who has it under a spell knows his business, and being determined to keep his island for himself changes its appearance as well as its location in order that his property may not be recognized nor appropriated.

In Galway, the Enchanted Island has appeared in the mouth of Ballinaleame Bay, a local landlord at the time making a devout wish that it would stay there. The fishermen of Ballynaskill, in the Joyce Country, saw it about fifteen years ago, since when it appeared to the Innisshark islanders. The County Mayo has seen it, not only from the Achille Island cliffs, but also from Downpatrick Head; and in Sligo, the fishermen of Ballysadare Bay know all about it, while half the population of Inishcrone still remember its appearance about twenty years ago. The Inishboffin islanders in Donegal say it looked like their own island, "sure two twins could n't be liker," and the people on Gweebarra Bay, when it appeared there, observed along the shore of the island a village like Maas, the one in which they lived. It has also appeared off Rathlin's Island, on the Antrim coast, but, so far as could be learned, it went no further to the east, confining its migrations to the west coast, between Cork on the south and Antrim on the north.

Concerning the island itself, legendary authorities differ on many material points. Some hold it to be "a rale island sure enough," and that its exploits are due to "jommethry or some other inchantmint," while opponents of this materialistic view are inclined to the opinion that the island is not what it seems to be, that is to say, not "airth an' shtones, like as thim we see, but only a deludherin' show that avil sper'ts, or the divil belike, makes fur to desave us poor dishsolute craythers." Public opinion on the west coast is therefore strongly divided on the subject, unity of sentiment existing on two points only; that the island has been seen, and that there is something quite out of the ordinary in its appearance. "For ye see, yer Anner," observed a Kerry fisherman, "it's agin nacher fur a rale island to be comin' and goin' like a light in a bog, an' whin ye do see it, ye can see through it, an' by jagers, if it's a thrue island, a mighty quare wan it is an' no mishtake."

On so deep and difficult a subject, an ounce of knowledge is worth a pound of speculation, and the knowledge desired was finally furnished by an old fisherman of Ballyconealy Bay, on the Connemara coast, west of Galway. This individual, Dennis Moriarty by name, knew all about the Enchanted Island, having not only seen it himself, but, when a boy, learned its history from a " fairy man," who obtained his information from "the good people " themselves, the facts stated being therefore, of course, of indisputable authority, what the fairies did not know concerning the doings of supernatural and enchanted circles, being not worth knowing. Mr. Moriarty was stricken in years, having long given up active service in the boats and relegated himself to lighter duties on shore. He had much confidence in the accuracy of his information on the subject of the island, and a glass of grog, and " dhraw ov the pipe," brought out the story in a rich, mellow brogue.

" Faith, I 'm not rightly sure how long ago it was, but it was a good while an' before the blessed Saint Pathrick come to the counthry an' made Crissans av the haythens in it. Howandiver, it was in thim times that betune this an' Inishmore, there was an island. Some calls it the Island av Shades, an' more says its name was the Sowls Raypose, but it does n't matther, fur no wan knows. It was as full av payple as it could howld, an' cities wor on it wid palaces an' coorts an' haythen timples an' round towers all covered wid goold an' silver till they shone so ye cud n't see for the brightness.

"And they wor all haythens there, an' the king av the island was the biggest av thim, sure he was Satan's own, an' tuk delight in doin' all the bloody things that come into his head. If the waither that minded the table did annything to displaze him, he 'd out wid a soord the length av me arrum an' cut aff his head. If they caught a man shtaling, the king 'ud have him hung at wanst widout the taste av a thrial, ' Bekase,' says the king, says he, ' maybe he did n't do it at all, an' so he 'd get aff, so up wid him,' an' so they 'd do. He had more than a hunderd wives, ginerally spakin', but he was n't throubled in the laste be their clack, for whin wan had too much blasthogue in her jaw, or begun gostherin' at him, he cut aff her head an' said, beways av a joke, that 'that's the only cure fur a woman's tongue.' An' all the time, from sun to sun, he was cursin' an' howlin' wid rage, so as I'm sure yer Anner would n't want fur to hear me say thim blastphee-mies that he said. To spake the truth av him, he was wicked in that degray that, axin' yer pardon, the owld divil himself would n't own him.

"So wan time, there was a thunderin' phillaloo in the king's family, fur mind ye, he had thin just a hunderd wives. Now it's my consate that it's aisier fur a hunderd cats to spind the night in pace an the wan thatch than for two wim-min to dhraw wather out av the same well widout aitch wan callin' the other wan all the names she can get out av her head. But whin ye've a hunderd av 'em, an' more than a towsand young wans, big an' little, its aisey to see that the king av the island had plinty av use fur the big soord that he always kept handy to settle family dishputes wid. So, be the time the row I'm tellin' ye av was over an' the wimmin shtopped talkin', the king was a widdy-man just ten times, an' had only ninety wives lift.

"So he says to himself, 'Bedad, I must raycrout the force agin, or thim that's left 'ull think I cant do widout 'em an' thin there'll be no ind to their impidince. Begorra, this mar-ryin' is a sayrious business,' says he, sighin', fur he'd got about all the wimmin that wanted to be quanes an' did n't just know where to find anny more. But, be pickin' up wan here an' there, afther a bit he got ninety-nine, an' then cud get no more, an' in spite av sendin' men to ivery quarther av Ireland an' tellin' the kings' dawthers iverywhere how lone-some he was, an' how the coort was goin' to rack an' ruin en-tirely fur the want av another quane to mind the panthry, sorra a woman cud be had in all Ireland to come, fur they'd all heard av the nate manes he tuk to kape pace in his family.

"But afther thryin' iverywhere else, he sent a man into the Joyce Counthry, to a mighty fine princess av the Joyces. She did n't want to go at first, but the injuicemints war so shtrong that she could n't howld out, for the king sint her presints widout end an' said, if she 'd marry him, he 'd give her all the dimunds they cud get on a donkey's back.

"Now over beyant the Twelve Pins, in the Joyce Counthry, there was a great inchanter, that had all kinds av saycrets, an' knew where ye 'd dig for a pot av goold, an' all about doctherin', and cud turn ye into a pig in a minnit, an' build a cassel in wan night, an' make himself disappare when ye wanted him, an' take anny shape he plazed, so as to look to be a baste whin he was n't, an' was a mighty dape man entirely. Now to him wint the princess an' axed him phat to do, for she did n't care a traneen for the king, but 'ud give the two eyes out av her head to get the dimunds. The inchanter heard phat she had to say an' then towld her, 'Now, my dear, you marry the owld felly, an' have no fear, fur av he daars to touch a hair av yer goolden locks, I 'll take care av you an' av him too.'

"So he gev her a charm that she was to say whin she wanted him to come an' another wan to repate whin she was in mortial danger an' towld her fur to go an' get marr'ed an' get the dimunds as quick as she cud. An' that she did, an' at foorst the king was mightily plazed at gettin' her, bekase she was hard to get, an' give her the dimunds an' all she wanted, so she got on very well an' tuk care av the panthry an' helped the other wives about the coort.

"Wan day the king got up out av the goolden bed he shlept an, wid a terrible sulk an him, an' in a state av mind entirely, for the wind was in the aiste an' he had the roomytisms in his back. So he cursed an' shwore like a Turk an' whin the waither axed him to come to his brekquest, he kicked him into the yard av the coort, an' wint in widout him an' set down be the table. So wan av the quanes brought him his bowl av stirabout an' thin he found fault wid it. 'It's burned,' say he, an' threw it at her. Then Quane Peggy

Joyce, that had n't seen the timper that was an him, come in from the panthry wid a shmile an her face an' a big noggin o' milk in her hand. 'Good morrow to ye,' she says to him, but the owld vagabone did n't spake a word. 'Good morrow,' she says to him agin, an' thin he broke out wid a fury.

"'Howld yer pace, ye palaverin' shtrap. D' ye think I 'm to be deefened wid yer tongue? Set the noggin an the table an' be walkin' aff wid yerself or I 'll make ye sorry ye come,' says he.

"It was the first time he iver spake like that to her, an' the Irish blood ov her riz, an' in a minnit she was as mad as a gandher and as bowld as a lion.

"'Don't you daar to spake that-a-way to me, Sorr,' she says to him. 'I 'll have ye know I won't take a word av yer impidince. Me fathers wore crowns ages afore yer bogthrottin' grandfather come to this island, an' ivery wan knows he was the first av his dirthy thribe that had shoes an his feet.' An' she walked strait up to him an' folded her arrums an' looked into his face as impidint as a magpie. 'Don't think fur to bully me,' she says. 'I come av a race that niver owned a coward, and I would n't give that fur you an' all the big soords ye cud carry,' says she, givin' her fingers a snap right at the end av his nose.

"Now the owld haythen niver had anny wan to spake like that to him, an' at first was that surprised like as a horse had begun fur to convarse at him, no more cud he say a word, he was that full o' rage, and sat there, openin' and shuttin' his mouth an' swellin' up like he 'd burst, an' his face as red as a turkey-cock's. Thin he remimbered his soord an' pulled it out an' stratched out his hand fur to ketch the quane an' cut aff her head. But she was too quick for him entirely, an' whin he had the soord raised, she said the charm that was to purtect her, an' afore ye cud wink, there stood the blood-suckin' owld villin, mortified to shtone wid his arrum raised an' his hand reached out, an' as stiff as a mast.

"Thin she said the other charm that called the inchanter an' he come at wanst. She towld him phat she done an' he said it was right av her, an' as she was a purty smart woman he said he 'd marry her himself. So he did, an' bein' that the

island was cursed be rayzon av the king's crimes, they come to
Ireland wid all the payple. So they come to Connemara, an'
the inchanter got husbands fur all the king's wives an' homes
fur all the men av the island. But he inchanted the island
an' made it so that the bad king must live in it alone as long
as the sun rises an' sits. No more does the island stand still,
but must go thravellin' up an' down the coast, an' wan siven
years they see it in Kerry an' the next siven years in Donegal,
an' so it goes, an' always will, beways av a caution to kings
not to cut aff the heads av their wives."

HOW THE LAKES WERE MADE.

AMONG the weird legends of the Irish peasantry is found a class of stories peculiar both in the nature of the subject and in the character of the tradition. From the dawn of history, and even before, the island has been crowded with inhabitants, and as the centres of population changed, towns and cities were deserted and fell into ruins. Although no longer inhabited, their sites are by no means unknown or forgotten, but in many localities where now appear only irregular heaps of earth and stones to which the archæologist sometimes finds difficulty in attributing an artificial origin there linger among the common people tales of the city that once stood on the spot ; of its walls, its castles, its palaces, its temples, and the pompous worship of the deities there adored. Just as, in Palestine, the identification of Bible localities has, in many instances, been made complete by the preservation among the Bedouins of the Scriptural names, so, in Ireland, the cities of pagan times are now being located through the traditions of the humble tillers of the soil, who transmit from father to son the place-names handed down for untold generations.

Instances are so abundant as to defy enumeration, but a most notable one is Tara, the greatest as it was the holiest city of pagan Ireland. Now it is a group of irregular mounds that the casual observer would readily mistake for natural hills, but for ages the name clung to the place until at last the attention of antiquaries was attracted, interest was roused, investigation made, excavation begun, and the site of Tara made a certainty.

Not all ancient Irish cities, however, escaped the hand of time as well as Tara, for there are geological indications of great natural convulsions in the island at a date comparatively recent, and not a few of the Irish lakes, whose name is legion, were formed by depression or upheaval, almost within the period of written history. A fertile valley traversed by a stream, a populous city by the little river, an earthquake-upheaval lower down the watercourse, closing the exit from the valley, a rising and spreading of the water, an exodus of the inhabitants, such has undoubtedly been the history of Lough Derg and Lough Ree, which are but reservoirs in the course of the River Shannon, while the upper and lower Erne lakes are likewise simply expansions of the river Erne. Lough Neag had a similar origin, the same being also true of Loughs Allen and Key. The Killarney Lakes give indisputable evidence of the manner in which they were formed, being enlargements of the Laune, and Loughs Carra and Mask, in Mayo, are believed to have a subterranean outlet to Lough Carrib, the neighborhood of all three testifying in the strongest possible manner to the sudden closing of the natural outlet for the contributing streams.

The towns which at one time stood on ground now covered by the waters of these lakes were not forgotten. The story of their fate was told by one generation to another, but in

course of ages the natural cause, well known to the unfortu-
nates at the time of the calamity, was lost to view, and the
story of the disaster began to assume supernatural features.
The destruction of the city became sudden ; the inhabitants
perished in their dwellings ; and, as a motive for so signal an
event was necessary, it was found in the punishment of duty
neglected or crime committed.

Lough Allen is a small body of water in the County Leitrim, and on its shores, partly covered by the waves, are several evidences of human habitation, indications that the waters
at present are much higher than formerly. Among the peasants in the neighborhood there is a legend that the little valley once contained a village. In the public square there was
a fountain guarded by spirits, fairies, elves, and leprechawns,
who objected to the building of the town in that locality, but
upon an agreement between themselves and the first settlers
permitted the erection of the houses on condition that the
fountain be covered with an elegant stone structure, the basin
into which the water flowed from the spring to be protected
by a cover never to be left open, under pain of the town's destruction, " the good people being that nate an' clane that
they did n't want the laste speck av dust in the wather they
drunk. So a decree was issued, by the head man of the town,
that the cover be always closed by those resorting to the
fountain for water, and that due heed might be taken, children, boys under age, and unmarried women, were forbidden
under any circumstances to raise the lid of the basin.

For many years things went on well, the fairies and the
townspeople sharing alike the benefits of the fountain, till, on
one unlucky day, preparations for a wedding were going on
in a house close by, and the mother of the bride stood in ur-
gent need of a bucket of water. Not being able to bring it

herself, the alleged reason being " she was scholdin' the house in ordher," she commanded her daughter, the bride expectant, to go in her stead.

The latter objected, urging the edict of the head man already mentioned, but was overcome, partly by her mother's argument, that " the good people know ye 're the same as married now that the banns are cried," but principally by the more potent consideration, " Av ye hav n't that wather here in a wink, I 'll not lave a whole bone in yer body, ye lazy young shtrap, an' me breaking me back wid the work," she took the bucket and proceeded to the fountain with the determination to get the water and " shlip out agin afore the good people 'ud find her out." Had she adhered to this resolution, all would have been well, as the fairies would have doubtless overlooked this infraction of the city ordinance. But as she was filling the pail, her lover came in. Of course the two at once began to talk of the all-important subject, and having never before taken water from the fountain, she turned away, forgetting to close the cover of the well. In an instant, a stream, resistless in force, burst forth, and though all the married women of the town ran to put down the cover, their efforts were in vain, the flood grew mightier, the village was submerged, and, with two exceptions, all the inhabitants were drowned. The girl and her lover violated poetic justice by escaping; for, seeing the mischief they had done, they were the first to run away, witnessed the destruction of the town from a neighboring hill, and were afterwards married, the narrator of this incident coming to the sensible conclusion that " it was too bad entirely that the wans that got away were the wans that, be rights, ought to be droonded first."

Upper Lough Erne has a legend, in all important particulars identical with that of Lough Allen, the catastrophe being, however, in the former case brought about by the carelessness of a woman who left her baby at home when she went after water and hearing it scream, " as aven the best babies do be doin', God bless 'em, for no betther rayson than to lishen at thimselves," she hurried back, forgetting to cover the well, with a consequent calamity like that which followed similar forgetfulness at Lough Allen.

In the County Mayo is found Lough Conn, once, according to local story-tellers, the site of a village built within and around the enclosure of a castle. The lord of the castle, being fond of fish, determined to make a fish-pond, and as the spot selected for the excavation was covered by the cabins of his poorest tenants, he ordered all the occupants to be turned out forthwith, an order at once carried out " wid process-sarvers, an' bailiffs, an' consthables, an' sogers, an' polis, an' the people all shtandin' 'round." One of the evicted knelt on the ground and cursed the chief with " all the seed, breed and gineration av 'im," and prayed " that the throut-pond 'ud be the death av 'im." The prayer was speedily answered, for no sooner was the water turned into the newly-made pond, than an overflow resulted ; the valley was filled ; the waves climbed the walls of the castle, nor ceased to rise till they had swept the chief from the highest tower, where " he was down an his hard-hearted knees, sayin' his baids as fast as he cud, an' bawlin' at all the saints aither to bring him a boat or taiche him how to swim quick." Regard for the unfortunate tenants, however, prevented any interference by the saints thus vigorously and practically supplicated, so the chief was drowned and went, as the story-teller concluded, to a locality where he " naded more wather than he 'd left behind him, an' had the comp'ny av a shwarm av other landlords that turned out the poor to shtarve."

Lough Gara, in Sligo, flows over a once thriving little town, the City of Peace, destroyed by an overflow on account of the lack of charity for strangers. A poor widow entered it one night leading a child on each side and carrying a baby at her breast. She asked alms and shelter, but in vain; from door to door she went, but the customary Irish hospitality, so abundant alike to the deserving and to the unworthy, was lacking. At the end of the village " she begun to scraich, yer Anner,

wid that shtrength you 'd think she 'd shplit her troat." At this provocation, all the inhabitants at once ran to ascertain the reason of so unusual a noise, upon which, when they were gathered 'round her, the woman pronounced the curse of the widow and orphan on the people and their town. They laughed at her and returned home, but that night, the brook running through the village became a torrent, the outlet was closed, the waters rose, and "ivery wan o' them oncharitable blaggârds wor drownded, while they wor aslape. Bad cess to the lie that's in it, for, sure, there's the lake to this blessed day."

In County Antrim there lies Lough Neag, one of the largest and most beautiful bodies of water on the island. The waters of the lake are transparently blue, and even small pebbles on the bottom can be seen at a considerable depth. Near the southern end, a survey of the bottom discloses hewn stones laid in order, and careful observations have traced the regular walls of a structure of considerable dimensions. Tradition says it was a castle, surrounded by the usual village, and accounts for its destruction by the lake on this wise. In ancient times, the castle was owned by an Irish chief named Shane O'Donovan, noted for his bad traits of character, being merciless in war, tyrannical in peace, feared by his neighbors, hated by his dependents, and detested by everybody for his inhospitality and want of charity. His castle then stood by the bank of the lake, on an elevated promontory, almost an island, being joined to the mainland by a narrow isthmus, very little above the water level.

By chance there came into that part of Ireland an angel who had been sent from heaven to observe the people and note their piety. In the garb and likeness of a man, weary and footsore with travel, the angel spied the castle from the hills above the lake, came down, and boldly applied for a night's lodging. Not only was his request refused, "but the oncivil Shane O'Donovan set an his dogs fur to bite him." The angel turned away, but no sooner had he left the castle gate than the villagers ran 'round him and a contest ensued as to which of them should entertain the traveller. He made his choice, going to the house of a cobbler who was "that poor that he'd but the wan pitatee, and when he wanted

another he broke wan in two." The heavenly visitor shared
the cobbler's potato and slept on the cobbler's floor, "puttin'
his feet into the fire to kape thim warrum," but at daylight
he rose, and calling the inhabitants of the village, led them
out, across the isthmus to a hill near by, and bid them look
back. They did so, beholding the castle and promontory
separated from the mainland and beginning to subside into
the lake. Slowly, almost imperceptibly, the castle sank, while
the waters rose around, but stood like a wall on every side of
the castle, not wetting a stone from turret to foundation. At
length the wall of water was higher than the battlements, the
angel waved his hand, the waves rushed over the castle and
its sleeping inmates, and the O'Donovan inhospitality was
punished. The angel pointed to a spot near by, told the villagers to build and prosper there ; then, as the awe-stricken
peasants kneeled before him, his clothing became white and
shining, wings appeared on his shoulders, he rose into the
air and vanished from their sight.

Of somewhat different origin is the pretty Lough Derryclare,
in Connemara, south of the Joyce Country. The ferocious
O'Flaherty's frequented this region in past ages, and, with
the exception of Oliver Cromwell, no historical name is better
known in the west of Ireland than O'Flaherty. One of this
doughty race was, it seems, a model of wickedness. " He was
as proud as a horse wid a wooden leg, an' so bad, that, savin'
yer presince, the divil himself was ashamed av him." This
O'Flaherty had sent a party to devastate a neighboring village,
but as the men did not return promptly, he started with a
troop of horse in the direction they had taken. On the way
he was passing through a deep ravine at the bottom of which
flowed a tiny brook, when he met his returning troops, and
questioning them as to the thoroughness with which their

bloody work had been done, found, to his great wrath, that they had spared the church and those who took refuge in its sacred precincts.

"May God drownd me where I shtand," said he, "if I don't shlay thim all an the althar," and no doubt he would have done so, but the moment the words passed his lips, the rivulet became a seething torrent, drowned him and his men, and the lake was formed over the spot where they stood when the curse was pronounced. "An' sometimes, they say, that when the lake is quite shtill, ye may hear the groans av the lost sowls chained at the bottom."

The fairies are responsible for at least two of the Irish lakes, Lough Key and the Upper Lough Killarney. The former is an enlargement of the River Boyle, a tributary of the Shannon, and is situated in Roscommon. At a low stage of water, ruins can be discerned at the bottom of the river, and are reported to be those of a city whose inhabitants injudiciously attempted to swindle the "good people" in a land bargain. The city was built, it seems, by permission of the fairies, the understanding being that all raths were to be left undisturbed. For a long time the agreement was respected, fairies and mortals living side by side, and neither class interfering with the other. But, as the necessity for more arable land became evident, it was determined by the townspeople to level several raths and mounds that interfered with certain fields and boundary lines. The dangers of such a course were plainly pointed out by the local "fairy-man," and all the "knowledgable women" lifted their voices against it, but in vain; down the raths must come and down they came, to the consternation of the knowing ones, who predicted no end of evil from so flagrant a violation of the treaty with the fairies.

The night after the demolition of the raths, one of the

towns-men was coming through the gorge below the city, when, "Millia, murther, there wor more than a hundherd t'ousand little men in grane jackets bringin' shtones an' airth an' buildin' a wall acrass the glen. Begob, I go bail but he was the skairt man when he seen phat they done, an' run home wid all the legs he had an' got his owld woman an' the childher. When she axed him phat he was afther, he towld her to howld her whisht or he 'd pull the tongue out av her an' to come along an' not spake a word. So they got to the top o' the hill an' then they seen the wathers swapin' an the city an' niver a sowl was there left o' thim that wor in it. So the good people had their rayvinge, an' the like o' that makes men careful wid raths, not to displaze their betthers, for there 's no sayin' phat they 'll do."

The Upper Killarney lake was created by the fairy queen of Kerry to punish her lover, the young Prince O'Donohue. She was greatly fascinated by him, and, for a time, he was as devoted to her as woman's heart could wish. But things changed, for, in the language of the boatman, who told the legend, "whin a woman loves a man, she 's satisfied wid wan, but whin a man loves a woman, belike he 's not contint wid twinty av her, an' so was it wid O'Donohue." No doubt, however, he loved the fairy queen as long as he could, but in time tiring of her, "he concluded to marry a foine lady, and when the quane rayproached him wid forgittin' her, at first he said it was n't so, an' whin she proved it an him, faith he 'd not a word left in his jaw. So afther a dale o' blasthogue bechuxt thim, he got as mad as Paddy Monagan's dog when they cut his tail aff, an' towld her he wanted no more av her, an' she towld him agin for to go an' marry his red-headed gurrul, ' but mârk ye,' says she to him, ' ye shall niver resave her into yer cassel.' No more did he, for the night o' the weddin', while they were all dhrinkin' till they were ready to burst, in comes the waither an' says, 'Here's the wather,' says he. 'Wather,' says O'Donohue, 'we want no wather to-night. Dhrink away.' 'But the wather's risin',' says the waither. 'Arrah, ye Bladdherang,' says O'Donohue, 'phat d' ye mane be inthrudin' an agrayble frinds an such an outspishus occasion wid yer presince? Be aff, or be the powdhers o' war I'll wather ye,' says he, risin' up for to shlay the waither. But wan av his gintlemin whuspered the thruth in his year an' towld him to run. So he did an' got away just in time, for the cassel was half full o' wather whin he left it. But the quane did n't want to kill him, so he got away an' built another cassel an the hill beyant where he lived wid his bride."

Still another origin for the Irish lakes is found in Mayo, where Lough Carra is attributed to a certain "giont," by name unknown, who formerly dwelt in the neighborhood, and, with one exception, found everything necessary for comfort and convenience. He was a cleanly "giont," and desirous of performing his ablutions regularly and thoroughly. The streams in the neighborhood were ill adapted to his use, for when he entered any one of them for bathing purposes "bad scran to the wan that 'ud take him in furder than to the knees." Obviously this was not deep enough, so one day when unusually in need of a bath and driven desperate by the inadequacy of the means, "he spit an his han's an' went to work an' made Lough Carra. 'Bedad,' says he, 'I'll have a wash now,' an' so he did," and doubtless enjoyed it, for the lake is deep and the water clear and pure.

Just below Lough Carra is Lough Mask, a large lake between Mayo and Galway. Concerning its origin, traditionary authorities differ, some maintaining that the lake was the work of fairies, others holding that it was scooped out by a rival of the cleanly gigantic party already mentioned, a theory apparently confirmed by the fact that it has no visible outlet, though several streams pour into it, its waters, it is believed, escaping by a subterranean channel to Lough Corrib, thence to the sea. Sundry unbelievers, however, stoutly assert a conviction that " it's so be nacher entirely an' thim that says it's not is ignerant gommochs that don't know," and in the face of determined scepticism the question of the origin of the lake must remain unsettled.

Thus far, indeed, it is painful to be compelled to state that scarcely one of the narratives of this chapter passes undisputed among the veracious tradition-mongers of Ireland. Like most other countries in this practical, poetry-decrying age, the Emerald Isle has scientists and sceptics, and among the peasants are found many men who have no hesitation in proclaiming their disbelief in " thim owld shtories," and who even openly affirm that " laigends about fairies an' giants is all lies complately." In the face of this growing tendency towards materialism and the disposition to find in natural causes an explanation of wonderful events, it is pleasant to be able to conclude this chapter with an undisputed account of the origin of Lough Ree in the River Shannon, the accuracy of the information being in every particular guaranteed by a boatman on the Shannon, " a respectable man," who solemnly asseverated " Sure, that's no laigend, but the blessed truth as I'm livin' this minnit, for I'd sooner cut out me tongue be the root than desave yer Anner, when every wan knows there's not a taste av a lie in it at all."

" When the blessed Saint Pathrick was goin' through Ireland from wan end to the other buildin' churches, an' Father Malone says he built three hundherd an' sixty foive, that's a good manny, he come to Roscommon be the way av Athlone, where ye saw the big barracks an' the sojers. So he passed through Athlone, the counthry bein' full o' haythens entirely an' not av Crissans, and went up the Shannon, kapin' the river on his right hand, an' come to a big peat bog, that 's where the lake is now. There were more than a thousand poor oma-dhawns av haythens a-diggin' the peat, an' the blessed saint convarted thim at wanst afore he 'd shtir a toe to go anny furder. Then he built thim a church an the hill be the bog, an' gev thim a holy man fur a priest be the name o' Caruck, that I b'lave is a saint too or lasteways ought to be fur phat he done. So Saint Pathrick left thim wid the priest, givin' him great power on the divil an' avil sper'ts, and towld him to build a priest's house as soon as he cud. So the blessed Caruck begged an' begged as long as he got anny money, an' whin he 'd the last ha'penny he cud shtart, he begun the priest's house fur to kape monks in.

"But the divil was watchin' him ivery minnit, fur it made the owld felly tarin' mad to see himself bate out o' the face that-a-way in the counthry where he 'd been masther so long, an' he detarmined he 'd spile the job. So wan night, he goes to the bottom o' the bog, an' begins dammin' the shtrame, from wan side to the other, layin' the shtones shtrong an' tight, an' the wather begins a risin' an the bog. Now it hap-pened that the blessed Caruck was n't aslape as Satan thought, but up an' about, for he misthrusted that the Owld Wan was dodgin' round like a wayzel, an' was an the watch fur him. So when the blessed man saw the wather risin' on the bog an' not a taste o' rain fallin', ' Phat 's this ? ' says he. ' Sure it 's some o' Satan's deludherin'.'

"So down he goes bechuxt the hills an' kapin' from the river, an' comes up below where the divil was workin' away pilin' on the airth an' shtones. So he comes craipin' up on him an' when he got purty clost, he riz an' says, 'Hilloo, Nayber!' Now Belzebub was like to dhrop on the ground wid fright at the look av him, he was that astonished. But there was no gettin' away, so he shtopped on the job, wiped the shweat aff his face, an' says, 'Hilloo yerself.'

"'Ye 're at yer owld thricks,' says the blessed Caruck.

"'Shmall blame to me, that 's,' says Belzebub, 'wid yer churches an' saints an' convartin' thim haythens, ye're shpiling me business entirely. Sure, have n't I got to airn me bread?' says he, spakin' up as bowld as a cock, and axcusin' himself.

"At first the blessed Caruck was goin' to be rough wid him for shtrivin' to interfare wid the church an' the priest's house be risin' the wather on thim, but that minnit the moon shone out as bright as day an' he looked back an' there was the beautifulest lake he iver set his blessed eyes on, an' the church wid its towers riz above it like a fairy cassel in a dhrame, an' he clasped his hands wid delight. So Satan looked too an' was mortefied to death wid invy when he seen how he bate himself at his own game.

"So the blessed Caruck towld Belzebub to lave the dam where it was, an' then, thinkin' av the poor bog-throtters that 'ud nade the turf, he ordhered him beways av a punishmint, to dig all the turf there was in the bog an' pile it up on the hill to dhry.

"'Don't you lave as much as a speck av it undher wather,' says he to him, 'or as sure as I 'm a saint I 'll make ye repint it to the end o' yer snakin' life,' says he, an' thin stud on the bank an' watched the Owld Deludher while he brought out the turf in loads on his back, an' ivery load as big as the church, till the hape av sods was as high as a mountain. So he got it done be mornin', an' glad enough was the divil to have the job aff his hands, fur he was as wet as a goose in May an' as tired as a pedler's donkey. So the blessed Caruck towld him to take himself aff an' not come back : that he was mighty well plazed to do.

" That 's the way the lake come to be here, an' the blessed Caruck come well out o' that job, fur he sold the turf an' built a big house on the shore wid the money, an' chated the divil besides, Glory be to God, when the Owld Wan was thry-in' his best fur to sarcumvint a saint."

ABOUT THE FAIRIES.

THE Oriental luxuriance of the Irish mythology is nowhere more conspicuously displayed than when dealing with the history, habits, characteristics and pranks of the "good people." According to the most reliable of the rural "fairy-men," a race now nearly extinct, the fairies were once angels, so numerous as to have formed a large part of the population of heaven. When Satan sinned and drew throngs of the heavenly host with him into open rebellion, a large number of the less warlike spirits stood aloof from the contest that followed, fearing the consequences, and not caring to take sides till the issue of the conflict was determined. Upon the defeat and expulsion of the rebellious angels, those who had remained neutral were punished by banishment from heaven, but their offence being only one of omission, they were not consigned to the pit with Satan and his followers, but were sent to earth where they still remain, not without hope that on the last day they may be pardoned and readmitted to Paradise. They are thus on their good behavior, but having power to do infinite harm, they are much feared, and spoken of, either in a whisper or aloud, as the " good people."

Unlike Leprechawns, who are not considered fit associates for reputable fairies, the good people are not solitary, but quite sociable, and always live in large societies, the members of which pursue the coöperative plan of labor and enjoyment, owning all their property, the kind and amount of which are somewhat indefinite, in common, and uniting their efforts to accomplish any desired object, whether of work or play. They travel in large bands, and although their parties are never seen in the daytime, there is little difficulty in ascertaining their line of march, for, " sure they make the terriblest little cloud o' dust iver raised, an' not a bit o' wind in it at all," so that a fairy migration is sometimes the talk of the county. " Though, be nacher, they 're not the length av yer finger, they can make thimselves the bigness av a tower when it plazes thim, an' av that ugliness that ye 'd faint wid the looks o' thim, as knowin' they can shtrike ye dead on the shpot or change ye into a dog, or a pig, or a unicorn, or anny other dirthy baste they plaze."

As a matter of fact, however, the fairies are by no means so numerous at present as they were formerly, a recent historian remarking that the National Schools and societies of Father Mathew are rapidly driving the fairies out of the country, for " they hate larnin' an' wisdom an' are lovers av nacher entirely."

In a few remote districts, where the schools are not yet well established, the good people are still found, and their doings are narrated with a childlike faith in the power of these first inhabitants of Ireland, for it seems to be agreed that they were in the country long before the coming either of the Irishman or of his Sassenagh oppressor.

The bodies of the fairies are not composed of flesh and bones, but of an ethereal substance, the nature of which is not determined. " Ye can see thimselves as plain as the nose on yer face, an' can see through thim like it was a mist." They have the power of vanishing from human sight when they please, and the fact that the air is sometimes full of them inspires the respect entertained for them by the peasantry. Sometimes they are heard without being seen, and when they travel through the air, as they often do, are known by a humming noise similar to that made by a swarm of bees. Whether or not they have wings is uncertain. Barney Murphy, of Kerry, thought they had ; for several seen by him a number of years ago seemed to have long, semi-transparent pinions, " like thim that grows on a dhraggin-fly." Barney's neighbors, however, contradicted him by stoutly denying the good people the attribute of wings, and intimated that at the time Barney saw the fairies he was too drunk to distinguish a pair of wings from a pair of legs, so this branch of the subject must remain in doubt.

With regard to their dress, the testimony is undisputed. Young lady fairies wear pure white robes and usually allow their hair to flow loosely over their shoulders; while fairy matrons bind up their tresses in a coil on the top or back of the head, also surrounding the temples with a golden band. Young gentlemen elves wear green jackets, with white breeches and stockings; and when a fairy of either sex has need of a cap or head-covering, the flower of the fox-glove is brought into requisition.

Male fairies are perfect in all military exercises, for, like the other inhabitants of Ireland, fairies are divided into factions, the objects of contention not, in most cases, being definitely known. In Kerry, a number of years ago, there was a great battle among the fairies, one party inhabiting a rath or sepulchral mound, the other an unused and lonely graveyard. Paddy O'Donohue was the sole witness of this encounter, the narrative being in his own words.

"I was lyin' be the road, bein' on me way home an' tired wid the walkin'. A bright moon was out that night, an' I heard a noise like a million av sogers, thrampin' on the road, so I riz me an' looked, an' the way was full av little men, the length o' me hand, wid grane coats on, an' all in rows like wan o' the ridgmints; aitch wid a pike on his showldher an' a shield on his arrum. Wan was in front, beway he was the ginral, walkin' wid his chin up as proud as a paycock. Jagers, but I was skairt an' prayed fasther than iver I did in me life, for it was too clost to me entirely they wor for comfort or convaynience aither. But they all went by, sorra the wan o' thim turnin' his head to raygard me at all, Glory be to God for that same; so they left me. Afther they were clane gone by, I had curosity for to see phat they were afther, so I folly'd thim, a good bit aff, an' ready to jump an' run like a hare at the laste noise, for I was afeared if they caught me at it, they 'd make a pig o' me at wanst or change me into a baste complately. They marched into the field bechuxt the grave-yard an' the rath, an' there was another army there wid red coats, from the graveyard, an' the two armies had the biggest fight ye iver seen, the granes agin the reds. Afther lookin' on a bit, I got axcited, for the granes were batin' the reds like blazes, an' I up an' give a whilloo an' called out, 'At 'em agin! Don't lave wan o' the blaggards!' An' wid that word, the sight left me eyes an' I remimber no more till mornin', an' there was I, layin' on the road where I seen thim, as shtiff as a crutch."

The homes of the fairies are commonly in raths, tumuli of

the pagan days of Ireland, and, on this account, raths are much dreaded, and after sundown are avoided by the peasantry. Attempts have been made to remove some of these raths, but the unwillingness of the peasants to engage in the work, no matter what inducements may be offered in compensation, has generally resulted in the abandonment of the undertaking. On one of the islands in the Upper Lake of Killarney there is a rath, and the proprietor, finding it occupied too much ground, resolved to have it levelled to increase the arable surface of the field. The work was begun, but one morning, in the early dawn, as the laborers were crossing the lake on their way to the island, they saw a procession of about two hundred persons, habited like monks, leave the island and proceed to the mainland, followed, as the workmen thought, by a long line of small, shining figures. The phenomenon was perhaps genuine, for the mirage is by no means an uncommon appearance in some parts of Ireland, but work on the rath was at once indefinitely postponed. Besides raths, old castles, deserted graveyards, ruined churches, secluded glens in the mountains, springs, lakes, and caves all are the homes and resorts of fairies, as is very well known on the west coast.

The better class of fairies are fond of human society and often act as guardians to those they love. In parts of Donegal and Galway they are believed to receive the souls of the dying and escort them to the gates of heaven, not, however, being allowed to enter with them. On this account, fairies love graves and graveyards, having often been seen walking to and fro among the grassy mounds. There are, indeed, some accounts of faction fights among the fairy bands at or shortly after a funeral, the question in dispute being whether the soul of the departed belonged to one or the other faction.

The amusements of the fairies consist of music, dancing,

FAIRY DANCE.

As played by a Connaught Piper, who learned it from "the Good People."

and ball-playing. In music their skill exceeds that of men, while their dancing is perfect, the only drawback being the fact that it blights the grass, "fairy-rings" of dead grass, apparently caused by a peculiar fungous growth, being common in Ireland. Although their musical instruments are few, the fairies use these few with wonderful skill. Near Coloney, in Sligo, there is a "knowlageable woman," whose grandmother's aunt once witnessed a fairy ball, the music for which was furnished by an orchestra which the management had no doubt been at great pains and expense to secure and instruct.

"It was the cutest sight alive. There was a place for thim to shtand on, an' a wondherful big fiddle av the size ye cud slape in it, that was played be a monsthrous frog, an' two little fiddles, that two kittens fiddled on, an' two big drums, baten be cats, an' two trumpets, played be fat pigs. All round the fairies were dancin' like angels, the fireflies givin' thim light to see by, an' the moonbames shinin' on the lake, for it was be the shore it was, an' if ye don't belave it, the glen's still there, that they call the fairy glen to this blessed day."

The fairies do much singing, seldom, however, save in chorus, and their songs were formerly more frequently heard than at present. Even now a belated peasant, who has been at a wake, or is coming home from a fair, in passing a rath will sometimes hear the soft strains of their voices in the distance, and will hurry away lest they discover his presence and be angry at the intrusion on their privacy. When in unusually good spirits they will sometimes admit a mortal to their revels, but if he speaks, the scene at once vanishes, he becomes insensible, and generally finds himself by the roadside the next morning, "wid that degray av pains in his arrums an' legs an' back, that if sixteen thousand divils were afther him, he cud n't stir a toe to save the sowl av him, that's phat the fairies

do be pinchin' an' punchin' him for comin' on them an'
shpakin' out loud."

Kindly disposed fairies often take great pleasure in assisting
those who treat them with proper respect, and as the favors always take a practical form, there is sometimes a business value
in the show of reverence for them.   There was Barney Noonan,
of the County Leitrim, for instance, " An' sorra a betther boy
was in the county than Barney.   He 'd work as reg'lar as a
pump, an' liked a bit av divarshun as well as annybody when
he 'd time for it, that was n't aften, to be sure, but small
blame to him, for he was n't rich be no manner o' manes.
He 'd a power av ragârd av the good people, an' when he
wint be the rath beyant his field, he 'd pull aff his caubeen an'
take the dudheen out av his mouth, as p'lite as a dancin'
masther, an' say, ' God save ye, ladies an' gintlemen,' that the
good people always heard though they niver showed thimselves to him.   He 'd a bit o' bog, that the hay was on, an'
afther cuttin' it, he left it for to dhry, an' the sun come out
beautiful an' in a day or so the hay was as dhry as powdher
an' ready to put away.

" So Barney was goin' to put it up, but, it bein' the day av
the fair, he thought he 'd take the calf an' sell it, an' so he
did, an' comin' up wid the boys, he stayed over his time, bein'
hindhered wid dhrinkin' an' dancin' an' palaverin' at the gurls,
so it was afther dark when he got home an' the night as black
as a crow, the clouds gatherin' on the tops av the mountains
like avil sper'ts an' crapin' down into the glens like disthroyin' angels, an' the wind howlin' like tin thousand Banshees, but Barney did n't mind it all wan copper, bein' glori-
fied wid the dhrink he 'd had.   So the hay niver enthered the
head av him, but in he wint an' tumbled in bed an' was shnorin' like a horse in two minnits, for he was a bach'ler, God

bless him, an' had no wife to gosther him an' ax him where he'd been, an' phat he'd been at, an' make him tell a hunderd lies about not gettin' home afore. So it came on to thunder an' lighten like as all the avil daymons in the univarse were fightin' wid cannons in the shky, an' by an' by there was a clap loud enough to shplit yer skull an' Barney woke up.

" ' Tattheration to me,' says he to himself, ' it 's goin' for to rain an' me hay on the ground. Phat 'll I do ? ' says he.

" So he rowled over on the bed an' looked out av a crack for to see if it was ralely rainin'. An' there was the biggest crowd he iver seen av little men an' wimmin. They 'd built a row o' fires from the cow-house to the bog an' were comin' in a shtring like the cows goin' home, aitch wan wid his two arrums full o' hay. Some were in the cow-house, resayvin' the hay; some were in the field, rakin' the hay together; an' some were shtandin' wid their hands in their pockets beways they were the bosses, tellin' the rest for to make haste. An' so they did, for every wan run like he was afther goin' for the docther, an' brought a load an' hurried back for more.

" Barney looked through the crack at thim a crossin' himself ivery minnit wid admiration for the shpeed they had. ' God be good to me,' says he to himself, ' 't is not ivery gossoon in Leitrim that 's got haymakers like thim,' only he never spake a word out loud, for he knewn very well the good people 'ud n't like it. So they brought in all the hay an' put it in the house an' thin let the fires go out an' made another big fire in front o' the dure, an' begun to dance round it wid the swatest music Barney iver heard.

" Now be this time he 'd got up an' feelin' aisey in his mind about the hay, begun to be very merry. He looked on through the dure at thim dancin', an' by an' by they brought out a jug wid little tumblers and begun to drink summat that

they poured out o' the jug.   If Barney had the sense av a
herrin', he 'd a kept shtill an' let thim dhrink their fill widout
openin' the big mouth av him, bein' that he was as full as a
goose himself an' naded no more; but when he seen the jug
an' the tumblers an' the fairies drinkin' away wid all their
mights, he got mad an' bellered out like a bull, 'Arra-a-a-h
now, ye little attomies, is it dhrinkin' ye are, an' never givin'
a sup to a thirsty mortial that always thrates yez as well as
he knows how,' and immejitly the fairies, an'the fire, an' the
jug all wint out av his sight, an' he to bed agin in a timper.
While he was layin' there, he thought he heard talkin' an' a
cugger-mugger goin' on, but when he peeped out agin, sorra
a thing did he see but the black night an' the rain comin'
down an' aitch dhrop the full av a wather-noggin. So he wint
to slape, continted that the hay was in, but not plazed that
the good people 'ud be pigs entirely, to be afther dhrinkin'
undher his eyes an' not offer him a taste, no, not so much as
a shmell at the jug.

 "In the mornin' up he gets an' out for to look at the hay
an' see if the fairies put it in right, for he says, 'It 's a job
they 're not used to.'   So he looked in the cow-house an'
thought the eyes 'ud lave him when there was n't a shtraw in
the house at all.   'Holy Moses,' says he, 'phat have they
done wid it ? ' an' he could n't consave phat had gone wid the
hay.   So he looked in the field an' it was all there ; bad luck
to the bit av it had the fairies left in the house at all, but
when he shouted at thim, they got tarin' mad an' took all the
hay back agin to the bog, puttin' every shtraw where Barney
laid it, an' it was as wet as a drownded cat.   But it was a les-
son to him he niver forgot, an' I go bail that the next time
the fairies help him in wid his hay he 'll kape shtill an' let
thim dhrink thimselves to death if they plaze widout sayin' a
word."

The good people have the family relations of husband and wife, parent and child, and although it is darkly hinted by some that fairy husbands and wives have as many little disagreements as are found in mortal households, "for, sure a woman's tongue is longer than a man's patience," and "a husband is bound for to be gosthered day in an' day out, for a woman's jaw is sharpened on the divil's grindshtone," yet opinions unfavorable to married happiness among the fairies are not generally received. On the contrary, it is believed that married life in fairy circles is regulated on the basis of the absolute submission of the wife to the husband. As this point was elucidated by a Donegal woman, "They 're wan, that 's the husband an' the wife, but he 's more the wan than she is."

The love of children is one of the most prominent traits of fairy character, but as it manifests itself by stealing beautiful babes, replacing them by young Leprechawns, the fairies are much dreaded by west coast mothers, and many precautions are taken against the elves. Thefts of this kind now rarely occur, but once they were common, as "in thim owld times, ye cud see tin fairies where there is n't wan now, be razon o' thim lavin' the counthry."

A notable case of baby stealing occurred in the family of Termon Magrath, who had a castle, now in picturesque ruins, on the shore of Lough Erne, in the County Donegal. The narrator of the incident was "a knowledgable woman," who dwelt in an apology for a cabin, a thatched shed placed against the precipitous side of the glen almost beneath the castle. The wretched shelter was nearly concealed from view by the overhanging branches of a large tree and by thick undergrowth, and seemed unfit for a pig-pen, but, though her surroundings were poor beyond description, "Owld Meg," in the language of one of her neighbors, "knew a dale av fairies an' witches an' could kape thim from a babby betther than anny woman that iver dhrew the breath av life."   A bit

of tobacco to enable her to take a "dhraw o' the pipe, an' that warms me heart to the whole worruld," brought forth the story.

" It 's a manny year ago, that Termon Magrath wint, wid all his army, to the war in the County Tyrone, an' while he was gone the babby was born an' they called her Eva. She was her mother's first, so she felt moighty onaisey in her mind about her 's knowin' that the good people do be always afther the first wan that comes, an' more whin it 's a girl that 's in it, that they thry to stale harder than they do a boy, bekase av belavin' they 're aisier fur to rare, though it 's mesilf that does n't belave that same, fur wan girl makes more throuble than tin boys an' is n't a haporth more good.

" So whin the babby was born they sent afther an owld struckawn av a widdy that set up for a wise woman, that knew no more o' doctherin' than a pig av Paradise, but they thought she could kape away the fairies, that 's a job that takes no ind av knowledge in thim that thries it. But the poor owld woman did the best she knew how, an' so, God be good to her, she was n't to be blamed fur that, but it 's the likes av her that do shame thim that 's larned in such things, fur they make people think all wise wimmin as ignerant as hersilf. So she made the sign o' the crass on the babby's face wid ashes, an' towld thim to bite aff its nails and not cut thim till nine weeks, an' held a burnin' candle afore its eyes, so it 'ud do the deeds av light an' not av darkness, an' mixed sugar an' salt an' oil, an' give it to her, that her life 'ud be swate an' long presarved an' go smooth, but the owld widdy forgot wan thing. She did n't put a lucky shamrock, that 's got four leaves, in a gospel an' tie it 'round the babby's neck wid a t'read pulled out av her gown, an' not mindin' this, all the rest was no good at all. No more did she tell the mother not to take her eyes aff the child till the ninth day ; afther that the fairies cud n't take it.

" So the nurse tuk the babby in the next room an' laid it

on the bed, an' wint away for a minnit, but thinkin' she heard it cry, back she come an' there was the babby, bedclothes an' all just goin' through the flure, bein' dhrawn be the fairies. The nurse scraiched an' caught the clothes an' the maid helped her, so that the two o' thim pulled wid all their mights an' got the bedclothes up agin, but while the child was out o' sight, the fairies changed it an' put a fairy child in its place, but the nurse did n't know phat the fairies done, no more did the owld struckawn, that shows she was an ignerant woman entirely. But the fairies tuk Eva away undher the lake where they trated her beautiful. Every night they gev her a dance, wid the loveliest music that was iver heard, wid big drums an' little drums, an' fiddles an' pipes an' thrumpets, fur such a band the good people do have when they give a dance.

"So she grew an' the quane said she should have a husband among the fairies, but she fell in love wid an owld Leprechawn, an' the quane, to sarcumvint her, let her walk on the shore o' the lake where she met Darby O'Hoolighan an' loved him an' married him be the quane's consint. The quane towld her to tell him if he shtruck her three blows widout a razon, she 'd lave him an' come back to the fairies. The quane gev her a power av riches, shape an' pigs widout number an' more oxen than ye cud count in a week. So she an' Darby lived together as happy as two doves, an' she had n't as much care as a blind piper's dog, morebetoken, they had two boys, good lookin' like their mother an' shtrong as their father.

"Wan day, afther they 'd been marred siventeen years, she an' Darby were goin' to a weddin,' an' she was shlow, so Darby towld her fur to hurry an' gev her a slap on the shouldher wid the palm av his hand, so she begun to cry. He axed her phat ailed her an' she towld him he 'd shtruck her the first av the three blows. So he was mighty sorry an' said he 'd be careful, but it was n't more than a year afther, when he was taichin' wan o' the boys to use a shtick, that she got behind him an' got hit wid the shillaly. That was the second blow, an' made her lose her timper, an' they had a rale quarl. So he got mad, sayin' that nayther o' thim blows ought to be counted, bein' they both come be accident. So he flung the shtick agin the wall, 'Divil take the shtick,' says he, an' went out quick, an' the shtick fell back from the wall an' hit her an the head.

'That's the third,' says she, an' she kissed her sons an' walked out. Thin she called the cows in the field an' they left grazin' an' folly'd her; she called the oxen in the shtalls an' they quit atin' an' come out; an' she shpoke to the calf that was hangin' in the yard, that they 'd killed that mornin' an' it got down an' come along. The lamb that was killed the day afore, it come; an' the pigs that were salted an' thim hangin' up to dhry, they come, all afther her in a shtring. Thin she called to her things in the house, an' the chairs walked out, an' the tables, an' the chist av drawers, an' the

boxes, all o' thim put out legs like bastes an' come along, wid
the pots an' pans, an' gridiron, an' buckets, an' noggins, an'
kish, lavin' the house as bare as a 'victed tinant's, an' all afther her to the lake, where they wint undher an' disappared,
an' have n't been seen be man or mortial to this blessed day.

"Now, there 's thim that says the shtory aint thrue, fur,
says they, how 'ud a woman do such a thrick as go aff that a
way an' take ivery thing she had, just bekase av her husband
hittin' her be accident thim three times. But thim that says
it forgits that she was a young wan, aven if she did have
thim boys I was afther tellin' ye av, an' faith, it 's no lie I 'm
sayin', that it 's not in the power av the angels o' God to be
knowin' phat a young wan 'ull be doin'. Afther they get
owld, an' do be losin' their taythe, an' their beauty goes, thin
they 're sober an' get over thim notions; but it takes a dale av
time to make an owld wan out av a young wan.

"But she did n't forget the boys she 'd left, an' wanst in a
while she 'd come to the aidge av the lake whin they were
clost be the bank an' spake wid thim, fur aven, if she was
half a fairy, she 'd the mother's heart that the good God put
in her bosom; an' wan time they seen her wid a little attomy
av a man alang wid her, that was a Leprechawn, as they
knewn be the look av him, an' that makes me belave that the
rale rayzon av her lavin' her husband was to get back to the
owld Leprechawn she was in love wid afore she was marr'd
to Darby O'Hoolighan."

THE BANSHEE.

Although the Irish have the reputation of being grossly superstitious, they are not a whit more so than the peasantry of England, France, or Germany, nor scarcely as much addicted to superstitious beliefs and fancies as the lower class of Scottish Highlanders. The Irish imagination is, however, so lively as to endow the legends of the Emerald Isle with an individuality not possessed by those of most other nations, while the Irish command of language presents the creatures of Hibernian fancy in a garb so vividly real and yet so fantastically original as to make an impression sometimes exceedingly startling.

Of the creations of the Irish imagination, some are humorous, some grotesque, and some awe-inspiring even to sublimity, and chief among the last class is " the weird-wailing Banshee, that sings by night her mournful cry," giving notice to the family she attends that one of its members is soon to be called to the spirit-world. The name of this dreaded attendant is variously pronounced, as Banshee, Banshi, and Benshee, being translated by different scholars, the Female Fairy, the Woman of Peace, the Lady of Death, the Angel of Death,

SONG OF THE BANSHEE.

By a KERRY PISHOGUE.

the White Lady of Sorrow, the Nymph of the Air, and the
Spirit of the Air.   The Banshee is quite distinct from the
Fearshee or Shifra, the Man of Peace, the latter bringing
good tidings and singing a joyful lay near the house when un-
expected good fortune is to befall any or all its inmates.   The
Banshee is really a disembodied soul, that of one who, in life,
was strongly attached to the family, or who had good reason
to hate all its members.   Thus, in different instances, the
Banshee's song may be inspired by opposite motives.   When
the Banshee loves those whom she calls, the song is a low, soft
chant, giving notice, indeed, of the close proximity of the
angel of death, but with a tenderness of tone that reassures
the one destined to die and comforts the survivors; rather a
welcome than a warning, and having in its tones a thrill of
exultation, as though the messenger spirit were bringing glad
tidings to him summoned to join the waiting throng of his
ancestors.   If, during her lifetime, the Banshee was an enemy
of the family, the cry is the scream of a fiend, howling with
demoniac delight over the coming death-agony of another of
her foes.

In some parts of Ireland there exists a belief that the spirits of the dead are not taken from earth, nor do they lose all
their former interest in earthly affairs, but enjoy the happiness of the saved, or suffer the punishment imposed for their

sins, in the neighborhood of the scenes among which they lived while clothed in flesh and blood. At particular crises in the affairs of mortals, these disenthralled spirits sometimes display joy or grief in such a manner as to attract the attention of living men and women. At weddings they are frequently unseen guests; at funerals they are always present; and sometimes, at both weddings and funerals, their presence is recognized by aerial voices or mysterious music known to be of unearthly origin. The spirits of the good wander with the living as guardian angels, but the spirits of the bad are restrained in their action, and compelled to do penance at or near the places where their crimes were committed. Some are chained at the bottoms of the lakes, others buried under ground, others confined in mountain gorges; some hang on the sides of precipices, others are transfixed on the tree-tops, while others haunt the homes of their ancestors, all waiting till the penance has been endured and the hour of release arrives. The Castle of Dunseverick, in Antrim, is believed to be still inhabited by the spirit of a chief, who there atones for a horrid crime, while the castles of Dunluce, of Magrath, and many others are similarly peopled by the wicked dead. In the Abbey of Clare, the ghost of a sinful abbot walks and will continue to do so until his sin has been atoned for by the prayers he unceasingly mutters in his tireless march up and down the aisles of the ruined nave.

The Banshee is of the spirits who look with interested eyes on earthly doings; and, deeply attached to the old families, or, on the contrary, regarding all their members with a hatred beyond that known to mortals, lingers about their dwellings to soften or to aggravate the sorrow of the approaching death. The Banshee attends only the old families, and though their descendants, through misfortune, may be brought down from

high estate to the ranks of peasant-tenants, she never leaves
nor forgets them till the last member has been gathered to
his fathers in the churchyard. The MacCarthys, Magraths,
O'Neills, O'Rileys, O'Sullivans, O'Reardons, O'Flahertys, and
almost all other old families of Ireland, have Banshees,
though many representatives of these names are in abject
poverty.

The song of the Banshee is commonly heard a day or two
before the death of which it gives notice, though instances
are cited of the song at the beginning of a course of conduct
or line of undertaking that resulted fatally. Thus, in Kerry,
a young girl engaged herself to a youth, and at the moment
her promise of marriage was given, both heard the low, sad
wail above their heads. The young man deserted her, she
died of a broken heart, and the night before her death, the
Banshee's song, loud and clear, was heard outside the window
of her mother's cottage. One of the O'Flahertys, of Galway,
marched out of his castle with his men on a foray, and, as his
troops filed through the gateway, the Banshee was heard high
above the towers of the fortress. The next night she sang
again, and was heard no more for a month, when his wife
heard the wail under her window, and on the following day
his followers brought back his corpse. One of the O'Neills
of Shane Castle, in Antrim, heard the Banshee as he started
on a journey before daybreak, and was accidentally killed
some time after, but while on the same journey.

The wail most frequently comes at night, although cases are
cited of Banshees singing during the daytime, and the song is
often inaudible to all save the one for whom the warning is
intended. This, however, is not general, the death notice being for the family rather than for the doomed individual.
The spirit is generally alone, though rarely several are heard

singing in chorus. A lady of the O'Flaherty family, greatly beloved for her social qualities, benevolence, and piety, was, some years ago, taken ill at the family mansion near Galway, though no uneasiness was felt on her account, as her ailment

seemed nothing more than a slight cold. After she had re-mained in-doors for a day or two several of her acquaintances came to her room to enliven her imprisonment, and while the little party were merrily chatting, strange sounds were heard,

and all trembled and turned pale as they recognized the singing of a chorus of Banshees. The lady's ailment developed
into pleurisy, and she died in a few days, the chorus being
again heard in a sweet, plaintive requiem as the spirit was
leaving her body. The honor of being warned by more than
one Banshee is, however, very great, and comes only to the
purest of the pure.

The " hateful Banshee " is much dreaded by members of a
family against which she has enmity. A noble Irish family,
whose name is still familiar in Mayo, is attended by a Banshee
of this description. This Banshee is the spirit of a young girl
deceived and afterwards murdered by a former head of the
family. With her dying breath she cursed her murderer, and
promised she would attend him and his forever. Many years
passed, the chieftain reformed his ways, and his youthful
crime was almost forgotten even by himself, when, one night,
he and his family were seated by the fire, and suddenly the
most horrid shrieks were heard outside the castle walls. All
ran out, but saw nothing. During the night the screams continued as though the castle were besieged by demons, and the
unhappy man recognized, in the cry of the Banshee, the voice
of the young girl he had murdered. The next night he was
assassinated by one of his followers, when again the wild, unearthly screams of the spirit were heard, exulting over his
fate. Since that night, the " hateful Banshee " has never
failed to notify the family, with shrill cries of revengeful glad-
ness, when the time of one of their number had arrived.

Banshees are not often seen, but those that have made
themselves visible differ as much in personal appearance as in
the character of their cries. The " friendly Banshee " is a
young and beautiful female spirit, with pale face, regular,
well-formed features, hair sometimes coal-black, sometimes

THE "FRIENDLY BANSHEE." Page 114.

golden; eyes blue, brown, or black. Her long, white drapery falls below her feet as she floats in the air, chanting her weird warning, lifting her hands as if in pitying tenderness bestowing a benediction on the soul she summons to the invisible world. The "hateful Banshee" is a horrible hag, with angry, distorted features; maledictions are written in every line of her wrinkled face, and her outstretched arms call down curses on the doomed member of the hated race. Though generally the only intimation of the presence of the Banshee is her cry, a notable instance of the contrary exists in the family of the O'Reardons, to the doomed member of which the Banshee always appears in the shape of an exceedingly beautiful woman, who sings a song so sweetly solemn as to reconcile him to his approaching fate.

The prophetic spirit does not follow members of a family who go to a foreign land, but should death overtake them abroad, she gives notice of the misfortune to those at home. When the Duke of Wellington died, the Banshee was heard wailing round the house of his ancestors, and during the Napoleonic campaigns, she frequently notified Irish families of the death in battle of Irish officers and soldiers. The night before the battle of the Boyne several Banshees were heard singing in the air over the Irish camp, the truth of their prophecy being verified by the death-roll of the next day.

How the Banshee is able to obtain early and accurate information from foreign parts of the death in battle of Irish soldiers is yet undecided in Hibernian mystical circles. Some believe that there are, in addition to the two kinds already mentioned, "silent Banshees," who act as attendants to the members of old families, one to each member; that these silent spirits follow and observe, bringing back intelligence to the family Banshee at home, who then, at the proper seasons, sings her dolorous strain. A partial confirmation of this theory is seen in the fact that the Banshee has given notice at the family seat in Ireland of deaths in battles fought in every part of the world. From North America, the West Indies, Africa, Australia, India, China; from every point to which Irish regiments have followed the roll of the British drums, news of the prospective shedding of Irish blood has been brought home, and the slaughter preceded by a Banshee wail outside the ancestral windows. But it is due to the reader to state, that this silent Banshee theory is by no means well or generally received, the burden of evidence going to show that there are only two kinds of Banshees, and that, in a supernatural way, they know the immediate future of those in whom they are interested, not being obliged to leave Ireland for the purpose of obtaining their information.

Such is the wild Banshee, once to be heard in every part of Ireland, and formerly believed in so devoutly that to express a doubt of her existence was little less than blasphemy. Now, however, as she attends only the old families and does not change to the new, with the disappearance of many noble Irish names during the last half century have gone also their Banshees, until in only a few retired districts of the west coast is the dreaded spirit still found, while in most parts of the island she has become only a superstition, and from the majesty of a death-boding angel, is rapidly sinking to a level with the Fairy, the Leprechawn and the Pooka; the subject for tales to amuse the idle and terrify the young.

THE ROUND TOWERS.

AMONG the ruins spread everywhere over the island, relics of prehistoric Ireland are common, but wonderful as are many of these monumental remains of a people as mysterious as their own structures, none are more remarkable than the round towers, found in almost every locality of note either for its history or antiquities. The number of these towers was formerly very great, but from the ravages of time, the convenience of the structures as quarries of ready hewn stone, and intentional destruction by intolerant or thoughtless persons, they have gradually disappeared, until, at present, only eighty-three remain, of which seventeen are nearly perfect, the remainder being in a more or less advanced stage of dilapidation.

The round towers vary in height, those remaining perfect or nearly so being from seventy to two hundred feet, and from eighty to thirty feet in diameter at the base. The entrance is twelve to eighteen feet from the ground, the tower being divided into stories about ten feet high, each story lighted by a single window, the highest compartment having invariably four lancet windows opening to the cardinal points of the compass. The roof is conical, made of overlapping stone

slabs, and a circle of grotesquely carved heads and zigzag ornamentation is found beneath the projecting cornice. The
masonry is of hewn stone, but not the least regularity is ob-
servable in the size or shape of the blocks, some being very
large, others small, and every figure known to the geometri-
cian can be found in the stones of a single tower.

All towers still standing occupy sites noted as historical,
and evidence, sufficient to warrant the belief, can be adduced
to show that almost every historic spot on Irish soil once
boasted one or more of these interesting structures. The
existing towers are generally found close by the ruins of
churches, abbeys, or other ecclesiastical buildings, and the effect on the landscape of the masses of ruins, surmounted by a
single tall shaft, is often picturesque in the extreme. The
proximity of the tower to the church is so common as to lead
writers on Irish antiquities to conjecture that the former was
constructed by the monks who built the church; those advo-
cating the Christian origin of the round tower taking the
ground that it was built, either as a place of safe-keeping for
valuable property, as a belfry for the church, or for the purpose of providing cells for hermits.

No one of these suppositions is tenable. In the troublous
times of Ireland, and, unhappily, it has had scarcely any other
kind, the monasteries and ecclesiastical buildings of every
description were generally spared, even by the most ruthless
marauders; and, had this not been the case, those possessing
sufficient valuable property to attract the cupidity of the law-
less were far more likely to provide an inconspicuous hiding
place for their wealth than to advertise its possession by erect-
ing a tower which, from every direction, was invariably the
most conspicuous feature of the landscape. That the towers
were not intended for belfries is evident from the fact that,

in nearly every case, the churches close by are provided with bell-towers forming a part of the sacred edifice, which would not be the case if the round towers had been designed for the purpose of supporting bells. That they were not built for hermit-cells is apparent from the fact that hermit-caves and cells are abundant in Ireland, and, almost without exception, in secluded spots. No doubt, from time to time, some of the round towers were adapted to each of these uses, but, in every case, convenience was the motive, the monks and church-builders altering the existing structure to meet a pressing necessity. In fact, there is excellent reason for believing that the round towers were not built by the monks at all, the monastic writers being very fond of recording, with great particularity, what they built and how they built it, and in no passage do they mention the construction of a round tower. Whenever allusion is made to these structures, their existence is taken for granted, and several church historians who mention the erection of churches at the foot of a round tower demonstrate that this peculiar edifice antedates the introduction of Christianity into Ireland.

The round towers are indisputably of pagan origin, and of antiquity so great as to precede written history. There is no doubt that the early Irish were sun and fire worshippers, and many excellent reasons may be given for the belief that the round towers were built by the Druids for purposes of religion.

Every tower has an extensive view to the East, so as to command an early sight of the rising sun, the dawn being the favorite hour for celebrating sun-worship. Every tower contains, at its base, so extraordinary a quantity of ashes and embers as to compel the conviction that, in each, a sacred or perpetual fire was kept burning. In every locality where a round

tower stands, there linger among the peasantry traditions
pointing to a use sacred but not Christian.   Perhaps the most
significant indication of their former character as places sacred
to sun and fire-worship is found in the names by which, to
the present day, they are known among the common people.
The generic Irish name for the round tower is Colcagh, fire-
God ; but the proper names designating particular towers are
still more characteristic.   Turaghan, the Tower of Fire ;
Aidhne, the Circle of Fire ; Aghadoe, the Field of Fire ; Tegh-
adoe, the Fire House ; Arddoe, the Height of Fire ; Kennegh,
the Chief Fire ; Lusk, the Flame ; Fertagh, the Burial Fire
Tower ; Fertagh na Guara, the Burial Fire Tower of the Fire
Worshippers ; Gall-Ti-mor, the Flame of the Great Circle ;
Gall-Baal, the Flame of the Community ; Baal-Tinne, the Fire
of the Community, and many similar names, retain the memory and worship of the Druids when written records are silent
or wanting.

In addition to the significance contained in the names of
the towers, the hills, mountains, or islands on which they are
situated have, very frequently, designations conveying an allusion, either to the circle, a favorite and sacred figure in
Druidical holy places, or to the sun or fire worship.   Another
curious circumstance, still further identifying the round tower
with the rites of sun worship, is found in the fact that wher-
ever this form of religion has prevailed, it has been accompa-
nied by well or spring worship, and, generally, by the venera-
tion of the ox as a sacred animal.   Most of the Irish round
towers have near them springs or wells still regarded as holy,
and concerning which many tales of miraculous cures are told,
while in not a few instances there yet linger in the same
neighborhoods legends of sacred cows, usually the property
of some famous local saint or hero.

The round towers of Ireland are, in fact, a portion of a vast system of towers of identical construction, and by following the geographical course of these structures, the march of fire worship from the East may be determined with some accuracy. Pass from Ireland to Brittany, and there, in the mountainous or hilly districts, several towers are found exactly like those of Ireland. In the north of Spain several remain; in Portugal, one; in the south of Spain they are numerous. Opposite the Spanish coast, in the north of Africa, there are also many, being found in various places in Morocco, Algeria, Tunis, and Tripoli. In Sardinia, several hundred are still standing; and written testimony to the purpose for which they were erected is abundant among the Sardinian records. In Minorca, among many others, is the famous Tower of Allaior. The mountain districts of south Italy have numbers of them, and they are also found on several hills in Sicily. Malta has the Giant's Tower, in every particular of appearance and construction identical with the Tower of Cashel in Ireland. Cyprus has them, and they still remain in Candia and on the coast of Asia Minor. In Palestine none have yet been found, or at least have not been recorded by travellers or surveyors; a fact that may, perhaps, be fully accounted for by the zeal of the Hebrews in destroying every vestige of Canaanitish idolatry; but, with some probability, it is conjectured that the " high places" broken down may have been towers of the sun, for the Canaanites were fire worshippers, and the name Baal is found alike in Palestine and Ireland.

In Syria, north of Palestine, they begin again; are found in Armenia, and in the Caucasus, so numerously as to crown almost every hill-top. East of the Caspian Sea they abound, and towards the centre of Asia as far as records of exploration and travel present reliable accounts of the country. Return-

ing to the shores of the Mediterranean, their existence on the
northern coast of Africa has been mentioned. In Arabia and
on the Egyptian shore of the Red Sea, they stand in considerable numbers, are found in Persia, Afghanistan, Beloochistan,
India, Ceylon, and Sumatra, in some places being still used, it
is said, for fire worship.

Throughout this vast extent of territory there is no material difference in the shape, appearance, or construction of the
round tower. In Sumatra and Java, as in Ireland, the door
is elevated, the building divided into stories; the walls are
constructed of many sided hewn stones, the upper story is
lighted by four windows looking to the cardinal points, the
cornice has the same kind of zigzag ornamentation, and the
roof is constructed in the same manner, of overlapping stones.
Even the names are nearly the same, for in India and Ireland
these buildings are Fire-Towers, Fire-Circles, or Sun-Houses.

Another bit of circumstantial evidence going to prove that
the round towers of Ireland were erected by a people having
the same religion and similar religious observances as the na-
tives of India is seen in the legends concerning the Indian
towers. In India, the local traditions tell how each of these
towers was built in one night by some notable character who
was afterwards buried in it. In Ireland, the same legend is
found; to the present day, the peasants of the neighborhood
telling with gusto the story of the tower being first seen in
the early morning, rising toward the sky on a spot where,
the evening before, no preparations for building had been
visible.

The Tower Tulloherin, for instance, was built in one night
by a monk who came to the neighborhood as a missionary.
Finding the people inhospitable, and unable to obtain lodging
for the night, he determined to remain, believing there could

not be found in Ireland a locality more in need of missionary work. So, on the evening of his arrival, he began to build, and by morning the tower was finished, and he took up his abode in it, preaching from its entrance to the crowds attracted by the fame of the miracle. The story of the Tower of Aghagower is similar, save in one particular, the saint in this case being aided by angels. Kilmackduagh was built in one night by angels without human assistance, the work being done at the solicitation of a saint who watched and prayed while the angels toiled.

Ballygaddy has a history somewhat less miraculous, the local peasant historian attributing its origin to a " giont " of the neighborhood. Having received a belligerent message from another " giont," he took a stand on Ballygaddy hill to watch for the coming of his antagonist, proposing, as the humble chronicler stated, " to bate the head aff the braggin' vagabone if he said as much as Boo." For seven days and nights he stood upon the hill, and at the end of that time, as may readily be believed, " his legs wor that tired he thought they 'd dhrop aff him." To relieve those valuable members he put up the tower as a support to lean on. The bellicose gigantic party who proposed the encounter finally came to time, and lovers of antiquities will be glad to learn that the tower-building giant " did n't lave a whole bone in the blaggârd's ugly carkidge." After the battle, the victor " shtarted for to kick the tower down," but, upon second thought, concluded to put the roof on it and " lave it for a wondher to thim little mortials that come afther him," for which consideration all honor to his memory.

The Tower Ardpatrick was, according to tradition, built under the auspices of Ireland's great saint, while the high tower on the Rock of Cashel is attributed, by the same authority, to Cormac Macarthy, king and archbishop of Cashel, who, being once engaged in hostilities with a neighboring potentate, needed a watch-tower, so summoned all his people, built the tower in one night, and, at sunrise, was able by its help to ascertain the location of the opposing army and so give it an overwhelming defeat. The Glendalough Tower was built by a demon at the command of Saint Kevin. This saint had conspicuously routed Satan on a previous occasion; so the arch-fiend and all the well-informed of his subjects kept at a safe distance from Glendalough, not caring to take any risks with so doughty a spiritual champion as Saint Kevin had proved himself to be in more than one encounter.

"But there was wan snakin' vagabone av a divil that come from furrin parts an' had n't heard the news about the saint, and the blessed saint caught him wan avenin' an' set him to work to build that tower. So the black rogue wint at it as hard as he knew how, an' was workin' away wid all the hands he had, as busy as a barmaid at a fair, thinkin' that afore sunrise he 'd have it so high it 'ud fall down be itself an' do the blessed saint not a ha'porth av good. But afther batin' owld Satan himself, Saint Kevin was n't to be deludhered be wan av his undershtrappers, an' was watchin' wid his two eyes every minnit o' the time, so whin the divil had the tower high enough, he threw his bishop's cap at it, an' it become shtone an' made the roof, so the omadhawn divil was baten at his own game."

The round tower is not without a touch of romance, one of the most notable structures, Monaster-Boice, having been built by a woman under peculiar circumstances. According to the legend, she was young, beautiful, and good, but though she ought to have been happy also, she was not, being persecuted by the attentions of a suitor chieftain, whose reputation must have been far from irreproachable, since he was characterized by the narrator of the story either as an "outprobrious ruffin," or "a sootherin', deludherin', murtherin' villin." Loving another chief who was a "gintleman entirely," and determined to escape from the obnoxious attentions of the

"ruffin" already mentioned, the lady, having learned that her disagreeable suitor had resolved to carry her off, employed two men to aid her the night before the proposed abduction, and, before morning, built the tower and took up her abode in the topmost chamber. In due season the chieftain came "wid a gang av thaves," but, disappointed in his "endayvor fur to

stale away her varchew," besieged the tower. Having taken
the precaution to provide a good supply of heavy stones, the
lady pelted her persecutors vigorously, " crackin' their haythen
shkulls the same as they wor egg-shells." Her heroism was
rewarded by her deliverance, for her lover, hearing of her
desperate situation, came to her relief and attacked the besiegers, so that " wid the lady flingin' shtones at the front o'
them, an' the other fellys beltin' 'em behind, they got disconsarted as not knowin' phat to do next, an' so they up's an'
runs like as tin thousand divils wor parshooin' afther thim.
So she was saved an' brought down, an' was married to the
boy av her heart the next Sunday, Glory be to God, an' that 's
the way the tower come to be built, an' shows that thim that
thries to marry a lady agin her will always comes to grief, fur
av she cant bate thim wid her tongue she can some other way,
fur a woman can always get phat she 's afther, an' bad luck
to the lie that 's in that."

THE POLICE.

URING the last few years, the most obviously conspicuous individual in Ireland is the policeman. Go where you will, if the policeman is not there before you, the reason is probably to be found in the fact that he has just been there and will likely return before you leave. In Dublin, Cork, Limerick, Athlone, Belfast, and other large cities and towns, the police are seen at every corner, singly, in pairs, and in groups. Fresh-looking police are going on duty; tired-out police are going home; clean, well-brushed police are starting to the country on horseback, having heard reports of rural disturbance; muddy police are coming in on jaunting-cars, with prisoners from the nearest eviction. Everywhere you meet them; young policemen, with fresh, rosy complexions; middle-aged policemen, with stern faces, bearing strong evidence of Irish pugilistic talent; old policemen, with deeply scarred and weather-beaten countenances, looking forward to speedy retirement and a moderate pension; they are in the city, in the village, on the high road, in the by-way, and on the mountain paths. At every railroad station they are to be seen in pairs, observing those who arrive and depart, and noting all that may seem suspicious in the appearance and actions of travellers.

As long as a stranger remains on the common, well-frequented tourist routes he escapes with a sharp glance of inspection, but let him leave the courses usually followed by travellers, or go into parts of the country not often visited by strangers, and he at once becomes an object of intense suspicion. You are driving along a retired country road; at the turn of the hill a policeman heaves in sight. He speaks pleasantly, and if nothing arouses his suspicion, he will pass on and you see him no more; but if the slightest distrust of you or your business finds lodgment in his mind, he marks you as a possible victim. He temporarily vanishes; look round as you proceed on your journey, and you may, by chance, catch a glimpse of him a mile or two away, peeping over a wall after you, but in the next village, where you stop for the night, he reappears, and the local policemen, after his coming, will be sure to observe you with some degree of attention. Leave your baggage in the public room of the inn and step out on the street. In comes the policeman, ascertains your name, takes a mental inventory of your effects, makes a note of the railway and hotel labels on your trunks, and goes away to report. A sharp detective is the policeman even in the country districts. He knows articles of American manufacture at a glance, and needs only to see your satchel to tell whether it came from America or was made in England. Talk with him, and he will chat cordially about the weather, the crops, the state of the markets, but all the time he is trying to make out who you are and what is your business. His eyes ramble from your hat to your shoes, and by the time the conversation is ended, he has prepared for the " sargeant " a report of your personal appearance and apparel. " Hat, English; coat, London-made; trousers, doubtful; shoes, American; party evidently an Irish Yankee, who might as well be looked after."

The Irish policeman, or "constable," as he is familiarly known on his native sod, is the son of a peasant. Finding life as a laborer or tenant in either case intolerable, he debated in his own mind the question whether he should emigrate to America, enlist in the British army, or apply for a place on the constabulary. The first step was, to him, the most acceptable, but he lacked the money to go; of the two courses left open, enlistment in the army was the more pleasant, since in Ireland the constabulary are almost entirely cut off from association with the people in a social or friendly way, a general belief prevailing that the Irishman who enters the police has deserted the cause of his country and entered the service of her deadliest foe. So the police are avoided by their former companions, shunned by old friends, and, lastly, what is of some consequence to a genuine Irishman, are given the cold shoulder by the ladies. To be sure, the Irishman who enlists in the British army would be treated in the same way at his old home, but as he usually leaves never to return, the case is materially different. Chance, or the obligation of supporting aged parents or a helpless family of young brothers and sisters, usually determines the question, and the young Irishman enters the constabulary, thenceforth to be a social leper, for the constable is hated by his countrymen with a hatred that knows no bounds.

From the day he puts on his neat blue uniform and saucerlike cap, the constable, in the troubled west coast counties, carries his life in his hand. Every hedge he scrutinizes with a careful eye; behind it may lurk an assassin. Every division wall is watched for suspicious indications, his alertness being quickened by the knowledge that he is guarding his own life.

He is compelled to undertake duties obnoxious to his own feelings and sense of justice, and to risk life and limb to carry out repugnant orders.   A bad year comes, a tenant is in arrears and cannot pay rent; the agent determines on an eviction and sends for the police.   The constables arrive in force, but the tenant has anticipated them and collected a crowd of

friends.   The hut is closed and barred, while inside are half a score of men and women, determined to resist as long as resistance is of any avail.

As soon as the police appear on the scene, a babel of Irish voices ensues and fearful curses and imprecations are hurled at all concerned in the eviction, succeeded by showers of stones from enthusiastic outside supporters of the cabin's defenders. The constables draw their clubs and make a rush, striking right and left at the heads of the crowd. A desperate battle ensues, in which the police are generally victorious, driving the rabble to a safe distance; then, leaving a portion of the force to keep them away, the remainder return to effect an entrance to the hut. A beam, handled by several pairs of strong arms, speedily demolishes the miserable pretence of a door, then in go the police, to be met with fists, clubs, stones, showers of boiling water, and other effective and offensive means of defence. After a stubborn contest the cabin is finally cleared; the furniture, if there be any, is set out in the road, the thatched roof torn off and scattered on the ground, the walls levelled, and the police, battered with sticks and stones, scalded, burned, return to headquarters with their prisoners. Not infrequently a policeman is killed on one of these evictionary expeditions, the defence of his slayers being generally grounded on the statement made in court in one instance of this kind near Limerick. " We niver intinded fur to· kill him at all, but his shkull was too thin entirely for a consthable, an' broke wid the batin' he was afther gettin'."

Firearms are not often used in these encounters between the police and the populace, for such battles always take place in daylight, and although, when an eviction promises to be of more than usual danger, the police carry rifles, strict orders are given not to use them save in dire extremity, and a policeman will be beaten almost to death without resorting to the use of his gun. On ordinary day-duty the police carry only a short club or revolver, hidden under the coat; but at night, the country constables are armed with rifle and bayonet, and patrol the roads in pairs, one walking on each side and as close as possible to the hedge or wall.

But in spite of the extraordinary difficulties and unceasing

dangers of his work the constable does his duty with scrupu-
lous exactness, and instances of treachery to the government
among the Irish constabulary are extremely rare. Indeed,
service in the constabulary is much sought for, and there are
always more applicants than vacancies. The physical stand
ard is so high that the police are the picked men of the
country, while the average grade of intelligence among them
is better than among the peasantry from whose ranks they
have come.

Ready as they are to go cheerfully on any service, however
laborious or perilous, there is one task which the constabulary
of the west coast hold in mortal detestation, and that is, an
expedition into the mountains to seize illicit stills and arrest
distillers of poteen. Such an enterprise means days and
nights of toilsome climbing, watching, waiting, and spying ;
often without result, and generally with a strong probability
that when the spot where the still has been is surrounded, the
police thinking they have the law breakers in a trap, the latter take the alarm, escape by some unknown path, leaving
nothing but " the pot and the smell " as reminiscences of
their presence and employment. The disappointing nature of
the duty is thus one good reason for the dislike felt for it by
the constables, but another is found in the unusual degree of
peril attending it, for in the mountains of Donegal, Mayo,
Galway, Clare, and Kerry, the distillers generally own firearms,
know how to use them, and feel no more compunction for
shooting a policeman than for killing a dog. The extremely
rugged character of the Mayo mountains, in particular, offers
many opportunities for the outlaws to practise their craft in
safety and secrecy, for, the whole neighborhood being on the
lookout for the enemy, there are always friends to give the
alarm. To hide the still in the ground or in a convenient

cave is the work of very few minutes, after which the distillers are quite at leisure and turn their attention to shooting at the police, a job attended with so little risk to themselves and so much discomfort to the constables that the latter frequently give up the chase on very slight provocation.

Near Lake Derryclare, in the Connemara district of Galway, and almost under the shadow of the Twelve Pins, there stands by the wayside a small rude monument of uncut stones, a mere heap, surmounted by a rough wooden cross. Such stone heaps as this are common on the west coast, and originate in the custom of making a family memorial, each member of the family, or, in some cases, each friend attending the funeral, contributing a stone to the rude monument. In some neighborhoods, every relative and friend casts a stone on the common pile whenever he passes the spot, so the heap is constantly growing. This particular monument in Connemara does not differ in any important respect from many others, but before it, in the summer of 1886, there knelt, all day long, an old peasant woman. Every morning she came from a hut in the glen near by and spent every hour of daylight in prayer before the wooden cross. It seemed to matter little to her whether it rained or the sun shone; in sunshine, the hood of her tattered cloak was thrown back and her white hair exposed, while the rain compelled her to draw the hood forward, but rain or shine she was always there, her lips silently moving as the beads slipped through her withered fingers, nor could any question divert her attention from her devotions. She never looked up, never took the slightest notice of remarks addressed to her, nor was she ever heard to speak aloud. Once a week provisions were sent to her house from the nearest police station; they were left within, and those who brought them went their way, for she gave them no word of

thanks, no look of gratitude; nor, for many years, had the
constables sent with the allowance made her by the government ventured to compel her to speak to them.

Her story was told by a Sergeant of Police, and formed a
painful illustration of the poteen trade in the mountains. In
the year 1850, while the country was still suffering from the
effects of the " starving time," she lived with her husband,
Michael O'Malley, and four sons, on a little farm near Lake
Derryclare. Year after year had the crops failed, but the little
family held together, faring, or rather starving, alike. In the
year mentioned, although the country in general was beginning
to recover from the famine, this part of Connemara was still
stricken, and the crop seemed likely again to fail. Starvation
stared the hapless family in the face. The boys were well
grown lads, accustomed to the hard life of peasants, and will-
ing to work if any could be found. All four left home, the
eldest going to Galway, the other three to the sea-shore, where
they found temporary employment in the fisheries. While so
engaged, they learned the secrets of the illicit distiller, and
having, in course of time, managed to procure a small still,
they returned home with it, and as the cabin was in a secluded quarter of a little frequented district, they persuaded
the old man to engage in the enterprise with them. The risk
of detection appeared so small, especially when compared with
the profits, that against the prayers and entreaties of the
woman, the still was set up in a retired spot near by and the
manufacture of the poteen begun in as large quantities as
their limited resources would allow. A number of years
passed, and, as their product found a ready sale in the neighborhood, the O'Malleys prospered as they had never done before, the boys married, and families grew around them.

The eldest brother, John O'Malley, having gone to Galway,

succeeded, by what he considered a great stroke of good fortune, in obtaining a place on the constabulary. The family at home knew nothing of him, nor had he communicated with them, for directly after his enlistment he was sent to the County Wexford on the opposite side of the island, and completely lost sight of his old home. Proving intelligent and capable, he was promoted, made a sergeant, and ordered to the County Galway. Immediately upon his arrival at his new post, a small village in Connemara, intelligence was brought of illicit distilling near the Twelve Pins, and O'Malley was ordered to proceed with a strong party of police to seize the still, and, if possible, arrest the criminals. The names of the offenders were not given, but the location of the glen where operations were carried on was described with such exactness that O'Malley, who knew every foot of ground in the vicinity, laid such plans as to render escape by the distillers a practical impossibility. Before dark one evening a party of twelve mounted constables armed with rifles started from Maume, at the head of Lough Corrib, travelled all night, and by morning Sergeant O'Malley had so posted his men round the glen that the arrest of the distillers was apparently a certainty. In the early dawn, before objects could be distinctly seen, several men were observed going into the glen, and, at a given signal, the police closed in on the little shanty where the still was in operation. A desperate fight ensued, and Sergeant O'Malley was shot dead by one of his brothers without knowing whose hand pointed the weapon. Two of the O'Malleys were killed by the police bullets, and a constable was mortally wounded. Michael and his remaining son were taken alive, afterwards tried for murder, when for the first time they learned that the dead Sergeant was their relative. Both were hanged, the singular circumstances of the crime for which they suffered attracting wide attention.

Mrs. O'Malley thus beheld herself, at a single blow, deprived of husband and four sons. For a time she was wildly demented, but the violence passed away, and as her clouded brain became calm, it was occupied by one idea, to the exclusion of all others, — prayer for the repose of her dead. The body of the Sergeant was buried near Maume, but O'Malley and his three sons were buried together under the cairn in a long disused churchyard through which the road passed, a churchyard like thousands more in Ireland, where the gravestones are hidden by the nettles and weeds. Thither, with a love stronger than death, goes the poor old woman every day, and, untiring in her devotion, spends her life reciting the prayers for the dead.

THE LEPRECHAWN.

VERY mythology has its good and evil spirits which are objects of adoration and subjects of terror, and often both classes are worshipped from opposite motives; the good, that the worshipper may receive benefit; the evil, that he may escape harm. Sometimes good deities are so benevolent that they are neglected, superstitious fear directing all devotion towards the evil spirits to propitiate them and avert the calamities they are ever ready to bring upon the human race; sometimes the malevolent deities have so little power that the prayer of the pious is offered up to the good spirits that they may pour out still further favors, for man is a worshipping being, and will prostrate himself with equal fervor before the altar whether the deity be good or bad.

Midway, however, between the good and evil beings of all mythologies there is often one whose qualities are mixed; not wholly good nor entirely evil, but balanced between the two, sometimes doing a generous action, then descending to a petty meanness, but never rising to nobility of character nor sinking to the depths of depravity; good from whim, and mischievous from caprice.

Such a being is the Leprechawn of Ireland, a relic of the pagan mythology of that country. By birth the Leprechawn

is of low descent, his father being an evil spirit and his
mother a degenerate fairy ; by nature he is a mischief-maker,
the Puck of the Emerald Isle. He is of diminutive size,
about three feet high, and is dressed in a little red jacket or
roundabout, with red breeches buckled at the knee, gray or
black stockings, and a hat, cocked in the style of a century
ago, over a little, old, withered face. Round his neck is an
Elizabethan ruff, and frills of lace are at his wrists. On the
wild west coast, where the Atlantic winds bring almost constant rains, he dispenses with ruff and frills and wears a frieze
overcoat over his pretty red suit, so that, unless on the lookout for the cocked hat, " ye might pass a Leprechawn on the
road and never know it 's himself that 's in it at all."

In Clare and Galway, the favorite amusement of the Leprechawn is riding a sheep or goat, or even a dog, when the
other animals are not available, and if the sheep look weary
in the morning or the dog is muddy and worn out with fa-
tigue, the peasant understands that the local Leprechawn has
been going on some errand that lay at a greater distance than
he cared to travel on foot. Aside from riding the sheep and
dogs almost to death, the Leprechawn is credited with much
small mischief about the house. Sometimes he will make the
pot boil over and put out the fire, then again he will make it
impossible for the pot to boil at all. He will steal the bacon-
flitch, or empty the potato-kish, or fling the baby down on
the floor, or occasionally will throw the few poor articles of
furniture about the room with a strength and vigor altogether
disproportioned to his diminutive size. But his mischievous
pranks seldom go further than to drink up all the milk or de-
spoil the proprietor's bottle of its poteen, sometimes, in spor-
tiveness, filling the bottle with water, or, when very angry,
leading the fire up to the thatch, and then startling the in-

mates of the cabin with his laugh as they rise, frightened, to put out the flames.

To offset these troublesome attributes, the Leprechawn is very domestic, and sometimes attaches himself to a family, always of the " rale owld shtock," accompanying its representatives from the castle to the cabin and never deserting them unless driven away by some act of insolence or negligence, " for, though he likes good atin', he wants phat he gets to come wid an open hand, an' 'ud laver take the half av a pratee that's freely given than the whole av a quail that's begrudged him." But what he eats must be specially intended for him, an instance being cited by a Clare peasant of a Leprechawn that deserted an Irish family, because, on one occasion, the dog having left a portion of his food, it was set by for the Leprechawn. "Jakers, 't was as mad as a little wasp he was, an' all that night they heard him workin' away in the cellar as busy as a nailer, an' a sound like a catheract av wather goin' widout saycin'. In the mornin' they wint to see phat he'd been at, but he was gone, an' whin they come to thry for the wine, bad loock to the dhrop he'd left, but all was gone from ivery cask an' bottle, and they were filled wid say-wather, beways av rayvinge o' phat they done him."

In different country districts the Leprechawn has different names. In the northern counties he is the Logheryman; in Tipperary, he is the Lurigadawne; in Kerry, the Luricawne; in Monaghan, the Cluricawne. The dress also varies. The Logheryman wears the uniform of some British infantry regiments, a red coat and white breeches, but instead of a cap, he wears a broad-brimmed, high, pointed hat, and after doing some trick more than usually mischievous, his favorite position is to poise himself on the extreme point of his hat, standing at the top of a wall or on a house, feet in the air, then

laugh heartily and disappear. The Lurigadawne wears an antique slashed jacket of red, with peaks all round and a jockey
cap, also sporting a sword, which he uses as a magic wand.
The Luricawne is a fat, pursy little fellow whose jolly round
face rivals in redness the cut-a-way jacket he wears, that always has seven rows of seven buttons in each row, though
what use they are has never been determined, since his jacket
is never buttoned, nor, indeed, can it be, but falls away from
a shirt invariably white as the snow. When in full dress he
wears a helmet several sizes too large for him, but, in general,
prudently discards this article of headgear as having a tendency to render him conspicuous in a country where helmets
are obsolete, and wraps his head in a handkerchief that he
ties over his ears.

The Cluricawne of Monaghan is a little dandy, being gor-
geously arrayed in a swallow-tailed evening coat of red with
green vest, white breeches, black stockings, and shoes that
" fur the shine av 'em 'ud shame a lookin'-glass." His hat is
a long cone without a brim, and is usually set jauntily on one
side of his curly head. When greatly provoked, he will sometimes take vengeance by suddenly ducking and poking the
sharp point of. his hat into the eye of the offender. Such
conduct is, however, exceptional, as he commonly contents
himself with soundly abusing those at whom he has taken offence, the objects of his anger hearing his voice but seeing
nothing of his person.

One of the most marked peculiarities of the Leprechawn
family is their intense hatred of schools and schoolmasters,
arising, perhaps, from the ridicule of them by teachers, who
affect to disbelieve in the existence of the Leprechawn and
thus insult him, for " it 's very well beknownst, that onless ye
belave in him an' thrate him well, he 'll lave an' come back

no more." He does not even like to remain in the neighborhood where a national school has been established, and as such schools are now numerous in Ireland, the Leprechawns are becoming scarce. "Wan gineration of taichers is enough for thim, bekase the families where the little fellys live forgit to set thim out the bit an' sup, an' so they lave." The few that remain must have a hard time keeping soul and body together for nowhere do they now receive any attention at meal-times, nor is the anxiety to see one by any means so great as in the childhood of men still living. Then, to catch a Leprechawn was certain fortune to him who had the wit to hold the mischief-maker a captive until demands for wealth were complied with.

"Mind ye," said a Kerry peasant, " the onliest time ye can ketch the little vagabone is whin he 's settin' down, an' he niver sets down axceptin' whin his brogues want mendin'. He runs about so much he wears thim out, an' whin he feels his feet on the ground, down he sets undher a hidge or behind a wall, or in the grass, an' takes thim aff an' mends thim. Thin comes you by, as quiet as a cat an' sees him there, that ye can aisily, be his red coat, an' you shlippin' up on him, catches him in yer arrums.

" ' Give up yer goold,' says you.

" ' Begob, I 've no goold,' says he.

" ' Then outs wid yer magic purse,' says you.

" But it 's like pullin' a hat full av taith to get aither purse or goold av him. He 's got goold be the ton, an' can tell ye where ye can put yer finger on it, but he wont, till ye make him, an' that ye must do be no aisey manes. Some cuts aff his wind be chokin' him, an' some bates him, but don't for the life o' ye take yer eyes aff him, fur if ye do, he 's aff like a flash an' the same man niver sees him agin, an' that 's how it was wid Michael O'Dougherty.

" He was afther lookin' for wan nigh a year, fur he wanted
to get married an' had n't anny money, so he thought the
aisiest was to ketch a Luricawne. So he was lookin' an'
watchin' an' the fellys makin' fun av him all the time. Wan
night he was comin' back afore day from a wake he 'd been
at, an' on the way home he laid undher the hidge an' shlept
awhile, thin riz an' walked on. So as he was walkin', he seen
a Luricawne in the grass be the road a-mendin' his brogues.
So he shlipped up an' got him fast enough, an' thin made him
tell him where was his goold. The Luricawne tuk him to
nigh the place in the break o' the hills an' was goin' fur to
show him, when all at wanst Mike heard the most outprobrious scraich over the head av him that 'ud make the hairs av
ye shtand up like a mad cat's tail.

" ' The saints defind me,' says he, ' phat 's that ? ' an' he
looked up from the Luricawne that he was carryin' in his
arrums. That minnit the little attomy wint out av his sight,
fur he looked away from it an' it was gone, but he heard it
laugh when it wint an' he niver got the goold but died poor,
as me father knows, an' he a boy when it happened."

Although the Leprechawns are skilful in evading curious
eyes, and, when taken, are shrewd in escaping from their cap-
tors, their tricks are sometimes all in vain, and after resorting
to every device in their power, they are occasionally compelled
to yield up their hidden stores, one instance of which was narrated by a Galway peasant.

" It was Paddy Donnelly av Connemara. He was always
hard at work as far as anny wan seen, an' bad luck to the day
he 'd miss, barrin' Sundays. When all 'ud go to the fair,
sorra a fut he 'd shtir to go near it, no more did a dhrop av
dhrink crass his lips. When they 'd ax him why he did n't
take divarshun, he 'd laugh an' tell thim his field was divar-

shun enough fur him, an' by an' by he got rich, so they knewn that when they were at the fair or wakes or shports, it was lookin' fur a Leprechawn he was an' not workin', an' he got wan too, fur how else cud he get rich at all."

And so it must have been, in spite of the denials of Paddy Donnelly, though, to do him justice, he stoutly affirmed that his small property was acquired by industry, economy, and temperance. But according to the opinions of his neighbors, " bad scran to him 't was as greedy as a pig he was, fur he knewn where the goold was, an' wanted it all fur himself, an' so lied about it like the Leprechawns, that 's known to be the biggest liars in the world."

The Leprechawn is an old bachelor elf who successfully resists all efforts of scheming fairy mammas to marry him to young and beautiful fairies, persisting in single blessedness even in exile from his kind, being driven off as a punishment for his heterodoxy on matrimonial subjects. This is one explanation of the fact that Leprechawns are always seen alone, though other authorities make the Leprechawn solitary by preference, he having learned the hollowness of fairy friendship and the deceitfulness of fairy femininity, and left the society of his kind in disgust at its lack of sincerity.

It must be admitted that the latter explanation seems the more reasonable, since whenever the Leprechawn has been captured and forced to engage in conversation with his captor he displayed conversational powers that showed an ability to please, and as woman kind, even among fairy circles, are, according to an Irish proverb, " aisily caught be an oily tongue," the presumption is against the expulsion of the Leprechawn and in favor of his voluntary retirement.

However this may be, one thing is certain to the minds of all wise women and fairy-men, that he is the " thrickiest little

divil that iver wore a brogue," whereof abundant proof is
given.   There was Tim O'Donovan, of Kerry, who captured a
Leprechawn and forced him to disclose the spot where the
"pot o' goold" was concealed.   Tim was going to make the
little rogue dig up the money for him, but, on the Leprechawn advancing the plea that he had no spade, released him,
marking the spot by driving a stick into the ground and plac-
ing his hat on it.   Returning the next morning with a spade,

the spot pointed out by the "little ottomy av a desaver" being in the centre of a large bog, he found, to his unutterable
disgust, that the Leprechawn was too smart for him, for in
every direction innumerable sticks rose out of the bog, each
bearing aloft an old "caubeen" so closely resembling his own
that poor Tim, after long search, was forced to admit himself
baffled and give up the gold that, on the evening before, had

been fairly within his grasp, if " he 'd only had the brains in his shkull to make the Leprechawn dig it for him, shpade or no shpade."

Even when caught, therefore, the captor must outwit the captive, and the wily little rascal, having a thousand devices, generally gets away without giving up a penny, and sometimes succeeds in bringing the eager fortune-hunter to grief, a notable instance of which was the case of Dennis O'Bryan, of Tipperary, as narrated by an old woman of Crusheen.

" It 's well beknownst that the Leprechawn has a purse that 's got the charmed shillin'. Only wan shillin', but the wondher av the purse is this : No matther how often ye take out a shillin' from it, the purse is niver empty at all, but whin ye put yer finger in agin, ye always find wan there, fur the purse fills up when ye take wan from it, so ye may shtand all day countin' out the shillin's an' they comin', that 's a thrick av the good peoples an' be magic.

" Now Dinnis was a young blaggârd that was always after peepin' about undher the hidge fur to ketch a Leprechawn, though they do say that thim that does n't sarch after thim sees thim oftener than thim that does, but Dinnis made his mind up that if there was wan in the counthry, he 'd have him, fur he hated work worse than sin, an' did be settin' in a shebeen day in an' out till you 'd think he 'd grow on the sate. So wan day he was comin' home, an' he seen something red over in the corner o' the field, an' in he goes, as quiet as a mouse, an' up on the Leprechawn an' grips him be the collar an' down's him on the ground.

" ' Arrah, now, ye ugly little vagabone,' says he, ' I 've got ye at last. Now give up yer goold, or by jakers I 'll choke the life out av yer pin-squazin' carkidge, ye owld cobbler, ye,' says he, shakin' him fit to make his head dhrop aff.

"The Leprechawn begged, and scritched, an' cried, an' said he was n't a rale Leprechawn that was in it, but a young wan that had n't anny goold, but Dinnis would n't let go av him, an' at last the Leprechawn said he 'd take him to the pot ov goold that was hid be the say, in a glen in Clare. Dinnis did n't want to go so far, bein' afeared the Leprechawn 'ud get away, an' he thought the divilish baste was afther lyin' to him, bekase he knewn there was goold closter than that, an' so he was chokin' him that his eyes stood out till ye cud knock 'em aff wid a shtick, an' the Leprechawn axed him would he lave go if he 'd give him the magic purse. Dinnis thought he 'd betther do it, fur he was mortially afeared the oudacious little villin 'ud do him some thrick an' get away, so he tuk the purse, afther lookin' at it to make sure it was red shilk, an' had the shillin' in it, but the minnit he tuk his two eyes aff the Leprechawn, away wint the rogue wid a laugh that Dinnis did n't like at all.

"But he was feelin' very comfortable be razon av gettin' the purse, an' says to himself, 'Begorra, 't is mesilf that 'll ate the full av me waistband fur wan time, an' dhrink till a stame-ingine can't squaze wan dhrop more down me neck,' says he, and aff he goes like a quarther-horse fur Miss Clooney's sheebeen, that 's where he used fur to go. In he goes, an' there was Paddy Grogan, an' Tim O'Donovan, an' Mike Conathey, an' Bryan Flaherty, an' a shtring more av 'em settin' on the table, an' he pulls up a sate an' down he sets, a-callin' to Miss Clooney to bring her best.

"'Where 's yer money?' says she to him, fur he did n't use to have none barrin' a tuppence or so.

"'Do you have no fear,' says he, 'fur the money,' says he, 'ye pinny-schrapin' owld shkeleton,' this was beways av a shot at her, fur it was the size av a load o' hay she was, an'

weighed a ton. 'Do you bring yer best,' says he. 'I'm a
gintleman av forchune, bad loock to the job o' work I'll do
till the life laves me. Come, jintlemin, dhrink at my axpinse.'
An' so they did an' more than wanst, an' afther four or five
guns apace, Dinnis ordhered dinner fur thim all, but Miss
Clooney towld him sorra the bit or sup more 'ud crass the lips
av him till he paid fur that he had. So out he pulls the magic purse fur to pay, an' to show it thim an' towld thim phat
it was an' where he got it.

"'And was it the Leprechawn gev it ye?' says they.

"'It was,' says Dinnis, 'an' the varchew av this purse is
sich, that if ye take shillin's out av it be the handful all day
long, they'll be comin' in a shtrame like whishkey out av a
jug,' says he, pullin' out wan.

"And thin, me jewel, he put in his fingers afther another,
but it was n't there, for the Leprechawn made a ijit av him,
an' instid o' givin' him the right purse, gev him wan just like
it, so as onless ye looked clost, ye cud n't make out the differ
betune thim. But the face on Dinnis was a holy show when
he seen the Leprechawn had done him, an' he wid only a
shillin', an' half a crown av dhrink down the troats av thim.

"'To the divil wid you an' yer Leprechawns, an' purses,
an' magic shillin's,' schreamed Miss Clooney, belavin', an' small
blame to her that's, that it was lyin' to her he was. 'Ye're
a thafe, so ye are, dhrinkin' up me dhrink, wid a lie on yer
lips about the purse, an' insultin' me into the bargain,' says
she, thinkin' how he called her a shkeleton, an' her a load fur
a waggin. 'Yer impidince bates owld Nick, so it does,' says
she; so she up an' hits him a power av a crack on the head
wid a bottle; an' the other felly's, a-thinkin' sure that it was
a lie he was afther tellin' them, an' he laving thim to pay fur
the dhrink he'd had, got on him an' belted him out av the

face till it was nigh onto dead he was.   Then a consthable comes along an' hears the phillaloo they did be makin' an' comes in.

"'Tatther an' agers,' says he, 'lave aff.   I command the pace.   Phat's the matther here?'

"So they towld him an' he consayved that Dinnis shtole the purse an' tuk him be the collar.

"'Lave go,' says Dinnis.   'Sure phat's the harrum o' getting the purse av a Leprechawn?'

"'None at all,' says the polisman, 'av ye projuice the Leprechawn an' make him teshtify he gev it ye an' that ye have n't been burglarious an' sarcumvinted another man's money,' says he.

"But Dinnis cud n't do it, so the cunsthable tumbled him into the jail.   From that he wint to coort an' got thirty days at hard labor, that he niver done in his life afore, an' afther he got out, he said he 'd left lookin' for Leprechawns, fur they were too shmart fur him entirely, an' it 's thrue fur him, bekase I belave they were."

THE HENPECKED GIANT.

N⁰ locality of Ireland is fuller of strange bits of fanciful legend than the neighborhood of the Giant's Causeway. For miles along the coast the geological strata resemble that of the Causeway, and the gradual disintegration of the stone has wrought many peculiar and picturesque effects among the basaltic pillars, while each natural novelty has woven round it a tissue of traditions and legends, some appropriate, others forced, others ridiculous misapplications of commonplace tales. Here, a long straight row of columns is known as the "Giant's Organ," and tradition pictures the scene when the giants of old, with their gigantic families, sat on the Causeway and listened to the music ; there, a group of isolated pillars is called the "Giant's Chimneys," since they once furnished an exit for the smoke of the gigantic kitchen. A solitary pillar, surrounded by the crumbling remains of others, bears a distant resemblance to a seated female figure, the "Giant's Bride," who slew her husband and attempted to flee, but was overtaken by the power of a magician, who changed her into stone as she was seated by the shore, waiting for the boat that was to carry her away. Further on, a cluster of columns forms the "Giant's Pulpit," where a presumably outspoken gigantic

preacher denounced the sins of a gigantic audience. The
Causeway itself, according to legend, formerly extended to
Scotland, being originally constructed by Finn Maccool and
his friends, this notable giant having invited Benandoner, a
Scotch giant of much celebrity, to come over and fight him.
The invitation was accepted, and Maccool, out of politeness,
built the Causeway the whole distance, the big Scotchman
thus walking over dryshod to receive his beating.

Some distance from the mainland is found the Ladies' Wishing Chair, composed of blocks in the Great Causeway, wishes
made while seated here being certain of realization. To the
west of the Wishing Chair a solitary pillar rises from the sea,
the "Gray Man's Love." Look to the mainland, and the
mountain presents a deep, narrow cleft, with perpendicular
sides, the "Gray Man's Path." Out in the sea, but unfortu-
nately not often in sight, is the "Gray Man's Isle," at present
inhabited only by the Gray Man himself. As the island,
however, appears but once in seventeen years, and the Gray
Man is never seen save on the eve of some awful calamity,
visitors to the Causeway have a very slight chance of seeing
either island or man. There can be no doubt though of the
existence of both, for everybody knows he was one of the
greatest of the giants during his natural lifetime, nor could
any better evidence be asked than the facts that his sweet-
heart, turned into stone, still stands in sight of the Causeway; the precipice, from which she flung herself into the
sea, is still known by the name of the "Lovers' Leap;" and
the path he made through the mountain is still used by him
when he leaves his island and comes on shore.

It is not surprising that so important a personage as the
Gray Man should be the central figure of many legends, and
indeed over him the story-makers seem to have had vigorous

competition, for thirty or forty narratives are current in the neighborhood concerning him and the principal events of his life. So great a collection of legendary lore on one topic rendered the choice of a single tradition which should fairly cover the subject a matter of no little difficulty. As sometimes happens in grave undertakings, the issue was determined by accident. A chance boat excursion led to the acquaintance of Mr. Barney O'Toole, a fisherman, and conversation developed the fact that this gentleman was thoroughly posted in the local legends, and was also the possessor of a critical faculty which enabled him to differentiate between the probable and the improbable, and thus to settle the historical value of a tradition. In his way, he was also a philosopher, having evidently given much thought to social issues, and expressing his conclusions thereupon with the ease and freedom of a master mind.

Upon being informed of the variety and amount of legendary material collected about the Gray Man and his doings, Barney unhesitatingly pronounced the entire assortment worthless, and condemned all the gathered treasures as the creations of petty intellects, which could not get out of the beaten track, but sought in the supernatural a reason for and explanation of every fact that seemed at variance with the routine of daily experience. In his opinion, the Gray Man is never seen at all in our day and generation, having been gathered to his fathers ages ago; nor is there any enchanted island; to use his own language, "all thim shtories bein' made be thim blaggârd guides that set up av a night shtringin' out laigends for to enthertain the quol'ty."

"Now, av yer Anner wants to hear it, I can tell ye the thrue shtory av the Gray Man, no more is there anny thing wondherful in it, but it's just as I had it from me grandfather, that towld it to the childher for to entertain thim.

"It's very well beknownst that in thim owld days there were gionts in plinty hereabouts, but they did n't make the Causeway at all, for that's a work o' nacher, axceptin' the Gray Man's Path, that I'm goin' to tell ye av. But ivery wan knows that there were gionts, bekase if there was n't, how cud we know o' thim at all, but wan thing's sartain, they were just like us, axceptin' in the matther o' size, for wan ov thim 'ud make a dozen like the men that live now.

"Among the gionts that lived about the Causeway there was wan, a young giont named Finn O'Goolighan, that was the biggest av his kind, an' none o' thim cud hide in a kish. So Finn, for the size av him, was a livin' terror. His little finger was the size av yer Anner's arrum, an' his wrist as big as yer leg, an' so he wint, bigger an' bigger. Whin he walked he carried an oak-tree for a shtick, ye cud crawl into wan av his shoes, an' his caubeen 'ud cover a boat. But he was a good-humored young felly wid a laugh that 'ud deefen ye, an' a plazin' word for all he met, so as if ye run acrass him in the road, he'd give ye 'good morrow kindly,' so as ye'd feel the betther av it all day. He'd work an' he'd play an' do aither wid all the might that was in him. Av a week day you'd see him in the field or on the shore from sun to sun as busy as a hen wid a dozen chicks; an' av a fair-day or av a Sunday, there he'd be, palatherin' at the girls, an' dancin' jigs that he done wid extrame nateness, or havin' a bout wid a shtick on some other felly's head, an' indade, at that he was so clever that it was a delight for to see him, for he'd crack a giont's shkull that was as hard as a pot wid wan blow an' all the pleasure in life. So he got to be four or five an' twinty an' not his betther in the County Antrim.

"Wan fine day, his father, Bryan O'Goolighan, that was as big a giont as himself, says to him, says he, 'Finn, me Laddybuck, I'm thinkin' ye'll want to be gettin' marr'd.'

" ' Not me,' says Finn.

" ' An' why not ?' says his father.

" ' I 've no consate av it,' says Finn.

" ' Ye 'd be the betther av it,' says his father.

" ' Faix, I 'm not sure o' that,' says Finn ; ' gettin' marr'd is like turnin' a corner, ye don't know phat ye 're goin' to see,' says he.

" ' Thrue for ye,' says owld Bryan, for he 'd had axpayrience himself, ' but if ye 'd a purty woman to make the stirabout for ye av a mornin' wid her own white hands, an' to watch out o' the dure for ye in the avenin',' an' put on a sod o' turf whin she sees ye comin', ye 'd be a betther man,' says he.

" ' Bedad, it 's not aisey for to conthravene that same,' says Finn, ' barrin' I might n't git wan like that. Wimmin is like angels,' says he. ' There 's two kinds av 'em, an' the wan that shmiles like a dhrame o' heaven afore she 's marr'd, is the wan that gits to be a tarin' divil afther her market 's made an' she 's got a husband.'

" Ye see Finn was a mighty smart young felly, if he was a giont, but his father did n't give up hope av gettin' him marr'd, for owld folks that 's been through a dale o' throuble that-a-way always thries to get the young wans into the same thrap, beways, says they, av taichin' thim to larn something. But Bryan was a wise owld giont, an' knewn, as the Bible says, there 's time enough for all things. So he quit him, an' that night he spake wid the owld woman an' left it wid her, as knowin' that whin it 's a matther o' marryin', a woman is more knowledgable an' can do more to bring on that sort o' mis'ry in wan day than a man can in all the years God gives him.

" Now, in ordher that ye see the pint, I 'm undher the need-

cessity av axplainin' to yer Anner that Finn did n't be no manes
have the hathred at wimmin that he purtinded, for indade he
liked thim purty well, but he thought he undhershtood thim
well enough to know that the more ye talk swate to thim, the
more they don't like it, barrin' they 're fools, that sometimes
happens. So whin he talked wid 'em or about thim, he spake
o' thim shuperskillious, lettin' on to despize the lasht wan o'
thim, that was a takin' way he had, for wimmin love thimselves
a dale betther than ye 'd think, unless yer Anner 's marr'd an'
knows, an' that Finn knew, so he always said o' thim the
manest things he cud get out av his head, an' that made thim
think av him, that was phat he wanted. They purtinded to
hate him for it, but he did n't mind that, for he knewn it was
only talk, an' there was n't wan o' thim that would n't give
the lasht tooth out av her jaw to have him for a husband.

"Well, as I was sayin', afther owld Bryan give Finn up,
his mother tuk him in hand, throwin' a hint at him wanst in
a while, sighin' to him how glad she 'd be to have a young
lady giont for a dawther, an' dhroppin' a word about phat an
iligant girl Burthey O'Ghallaghy was, that was the dawther
av wan o' the naburs, that she got Finn, unbeknownst to himself, to be thinkin' about Burthey. She was a fine young lady
giont, about tin feet high, as broad as a cassel dure, but she
was good size for Finn, as ye know be phat I said av him.
So when Finn's mother see him takin' her home from church
afther benediction, an' the nabers towld her how they obsarved
him lanin' on O'Ghallaghy's wall an' Burthey lightin' his
pipe wid a coal, she thought to herself, 'fair an' aisey goes
far in a day,' an' made her mind up that Finn 'ud marry Burthey. An' so, belike, he 'd a' done, if he had n't gone over,
wan onlucky day, to the village beyant, where the common
people like you an' me lived.

"When he got there, in he wint to the inn to get him his dhrink, for it 's a mishtake to think that thim gionts were all blood-suckin' blaggârds as the Causeway guides say, but, barrin' they were in dhrink, were as paceable as rabbits. So when Finn wint in, he says, 'God save ye,' to thim settin', an' gev the table a big crack wid his shillaylah as for to say he wanted his glass. But instead o' the owld granny that used for to fetch him his potheen, out shteps a nate little woman wid hair an' eyes as black as a crow an' two lips on her as red as a cherry an' a quick sharp way like a cat in a hurry.

"'An' who are you, me Dear?' says Finn, lookin' up.

"'I 'm the new barmaid, Sorr, av it 's plazin' to ye,' says she, makin' a curchey, an' lookin' shtrait in his face.

"'It is plazin',' says Finn. ''T is I that 's glad to be sarved be wan like you. Only,' says he, 'I know be the look o' yer eye ye 've a timper.'

"'Dade I have,' says she, talkin' back at him, 'an' ye 'd betther not wake it.'

"Finn had more to say an' so did she, that I won't throuble yer Anner wid, but when he got his fill av dhrink an' said all he 'd in his head, an' she kep' aven wid him at ivery pint, he wint away mightily plazed. The next Sunday but wan he was back agin, an' the Sunday afther, an' afther that agin. By an' by, he 'd come over in the avenin' afther the work was done, an' lane on the bar or set on the table, talkin' wid the barmaid, for she was as sharp as a thornbush, an' sorra a word Finn 'ud say to her in impidince or anny other way, but she 'd give him his answer afore he cud get his mouth shut.

"Now, be this time, Finn's mother had made up her mind that Finn 'ud marry Burthey, an' so she sent for the matchmaker, an' they talked it all over, an' Finn's father seen Burthey's father, an' they settled phat Burthey 'ud get an' phat

Finn was to have, an' were come to an agraymint about the match, onbeknownst to Finn, bekase it was in thim days like it is now, the matches bein' made be the owld people, an' all the young wans did was to go an' be marr'd an' make the best av it. Afther all, maybe that's as good a way as anny, for whin ye've got all the throuble on yer back ye can stagger undher, there's not a haporth o' differ whether ye got undher it yerself or whether it was put on ye, an' so it is wid gettin' marr'd, at laste so I'm towld.

"Annyhow, Finn's mother was busy wid preparin' for the weddin' whin she heard how Finn was afther puttin' in his time at the village.

"'Sure that won't do,' she says to herself; 'he ought to know betther than to be spendin' ivery rap he's got in dhrink an' gostherin' at that black-eyed huzzy, an' he to be marr'd to the best girl in the county.' So that night, when Finn come in, she spake fair an' soft to him that he'd give up goin' to the inn, an' get ready for to be marr'd at wanst. An' that did well enough till she got to the·marryin', when Finn riz up aff his sate, an' shut his taith so hard he bruk his pipe-stem to smithereens.

"'Say no more, mother,' he says to her. 'Burthey's good enough, but I wouldn't marry her if she was made av goold. Begob, she's too big. I want no hogs'ead av a girl like her,' says he. 'If I'm to be marr'd, I want a little woman. They're betther o' their size, an' it don't take so much to buy gowns for thim, naither do they ate so much,' says he.

"'A-a-ah, baithershin,' says his mother to him; 'phat d'ye mane be talkin' that-a-way, an' me workin' me fingers to the bone clanin' the house for ye, an' relavin' ye av all the coortin' so as ye'd not be bothered in the laste wid it.'

"'Shmall thanks to ye,' says Finn, 'sure isn't the coortin' the best share o' the job?'

" ' Don't ye mane to marry her ? ' says his mother.

" ' Divil a toe will I go wid her,' says Finn.

" ' Out, ye onmannerly young blaggârd, I 'd tell ye to go to the divil, but ye 're on the way fast enough, an' bad luck to the fut I 'll shtir to halt ye. Only I 'm sorry for Burthey,' says she, ' wid her new gown made. When her brother comes back, begob 't is he that 'll be the death av ye immejitly afther he dhrops his two eyes on ye.'

" ' Aisey now,' says Finn, ' if he opens his big mouth at me, I 'll make him wondher why he was n't born deef an' dumb,' says he, an' so he would, for all that he was so paceable.

" Afther that, phat was his mother to do but lave aff an' go to bed, that she done, givin' Finn all the talk in her head an' a million curses besides, for she was mightily vexed at bein' bate that way an' was in a divil av a timper along o' the house-clanin', that always puts wimmin into a shtate av mind.

" So the next day the news was towld, an' Finn got to be a holy show for the nabers, bekase av not marryin' Burthey an' wantin' the barmaid. They were afeared to say annything to himself about it, for he 'd an arm on him the thick o' yer waist, an' no wan wanted to see how well he cud use it, but they 'd whisper afther him, an' whin he wint along the road, they 'd pint afther him, an' by an' by a giont like himself, an uncle av him, towld him he 'd betther lave the counthry, an' so he thought he 'd do an' made ready for to shtart.

" But poor Burthey pined wid shame an' grief at the loss av him, for she loved him wid all the heart she had, an' that was purty big. So she fell aff her weight, till from the size av a hogs'ead she got no bigger round than a barrel an' was like to die. But all the time she kept on hopin' that he 'd come to her, but whin she heard for sartain he was goin' to lave the counthry she let go an' jumped aff that clift into the say an' committed shooicide an' drownded herself. She was n't turned into a pillar at all, that 's wan o' thim guides' lies; she just drownded like annybody that fell into the wather would, an' was found afther an' berrid be the fishermen, an' a hard job av it they had, for she weighed a ton. But they called the place the Lovers' Lape, bekase she jumped from it, an' lovin' Finn the way she did, the lape she tuk made the place be called afther her an' that 's razon enough.

"Finn was showbogher enough afore, but afther that he seen it was no use thryin' for to live in Ireland at all, so he got the barmaid, that was aiquel to goin' wid him, the more that ivery wan was agin him, that 's beway o' the conthrariness av wimmin, that are always ready for to do annything ye don't want thim to do, an' wint to Scotland an' was n't heard av for a long time.

"About twelve years afther, there was a great talk that Finn had got back from Scotland wid his wife an' had taken the farm over be the village, the first on the left as ye go down the mountain. At first there was no end av the fuss that was, for Burthey's frinds had n't forgotten, but it all come to talk, so Finn settled down quite enough an' wint to work. But he was an althered man. His hair an' beard were gray as a badger, so they called him the Gray Man, an' he 'd a look on him like a shape-stalin' dog. Everybody wondhered, but they did n't wondher long, for it was aisely persaived he had cause enough, for the tongue o' Missis Finn wint like a stame-ingine, kapin' so far ahead av her branes that she 'd have to shtop an' say 'an'-uh, an'-uh,' to give the latther time for to ketch up. Jagers, but she was the woman for to talk an' schold an' clack away till ye 'd want to die to be rid av her. When she was young she was a purty nice girl, but as she got owlder her nose got sharp, her lips were as thin as the aidge av a sickle, an' her chin was as pinted as the bow av a boat. The way she managed Finn was beautiful to see, for he was that afeared av her tongue that he dar n't say his sowl belonged to him when she was by.

"When he got up airly in the mornin', she 'd ax, 'Now phat are ye raisin' up so soon for, an' me just closin' me eyes in slape?' an' if he 'd lay abed, she 'd tell him to 'get along out o' that now, ye big gossoon; if it was n't for me ye 'd do nothin' at all but slape like a pig.' If he 'd go out, she 'd gosther him about where he was goin' an' phat he meant to do when he got there; if he shtayed at home, she 'd raymark that he done nothin' but set in the cabin like a boss o' shtraw. When he thried for to plaze her, she 'd grumble at him bekase he did n't thry sooner; when he let her be, she 'd fall into a fury an' shtorm till his hair shtud up like it was bewitched it was.

"She 'd more thricks than a showman's dog. If scholdin' did n't do for Finn, she 'd cry at him, an' had tin childher that she larned to cry at him too, an' when she begun, the tin o' thim 'ud set up a yell that 'ud deefen a thrumpeter, so Finn 'ud give in.

"She cud fall ill on tin minnits notice, an' if Finn was obsthreperous in that degray that she cud n't do him no other way, she 'd let on her head ached fit to shplit, so she 'd go to bed an' shtay there till she 'd got him undher her thumb agin. So she knew just where to find him whin she wanted him; that wimmin undhershtand, for there 's more divilmint in wan woman's head about gettin' phat she wants than in tin men's bodies.

"Sure, if iver annybody had raison to remimber the ould song, "When I was single," it was Finn.

"So, ye see, Finn, the Gray Man, was afther havin' the divil's own time, an' that was beways av a mishtake he made about marryin'. He thought it was wan o' thim goold bands the quol'ty ladies wear on their arrums, but he found it was a handcuff it was. Sure wimmin are quare craythers. Ye think life wid wan o' thim is like a sunshiny day an' it's nothing but drizzle an' fog from dawn to dark, an' it's my belafe that Misther O'Day wasn't far wrong when he said wimmin are like the owld gun he had in the house an' that wint aff an the shly wan day an' killed the footman. 'Sure it looked innycent enough,' says he, 'but it was loaded all the same, an' only waitin' for an axcuse to go aff at some wan, an' that's like a woman, so it is,' he'd say, an' ivery wan 'ud laugh when he towld that joke, for he was the landlord, 'that's like a woman, for she's not to be thrusted avin when she's dead.'

"But it's me own belafe that the most sarious mishtake av Finn's was in marryin' a little woman. There's thim that says all wimmin is a mishtake be nacher, but there's a big differ bechuxt a little woman an' a big wan, the little wans have sowls too big for their bodies, so are always lookin' out for a big man to marry, an' the bigger he is, the betther they like him, as knowin' they can manage him all the aisier. So it was wid Finn an' his little wife, for be hook an' be crook she rejuiced him in that obejince that if she towld him for to go an' shtand on his head in the corner, he'd do it wid the risk av his life, bekase he'd wanted to die an' go to heaven as he heard the priest say there was no marryin' there, an' though he didn't dare to hint it, he belaved in his sowl that the rayzon was the wimmin didn't get that far.

"Afther they'd been living here about a year, Finn thought he'd fish a bit an' so help along, considherin' he'd a big family an' none o' the childher owld enough for to work.

WHEN I WAS SINGLE.

1. When I was single   I lived at me aise,   Now I am married, I
2. First it is "Daddy, I want a pace av bread,"   Then it is "Daddy, I

have   a wife   to plaze,   Ten shmall chil - dher I
want   to go   to bed,"   Sure I wash thim   an dress thim

have tò maintain,   Jagers, don't I wish I was sin-gle   a-gain!
Put 'em all to bed,   Me wife is such a schold I wish that I   was dead.

So he got a boat an' did purty well an' his wife used to come acrass the hill to the shore to help him wid the catch. But it was far up an' down agin an' she 'd get tired wid climbin' the hill an' jawing at Finn on the way.

"So wan day as they were comin' home, they passed a cabin an' there was the man that lived there, that was only a ditcher, a workin' away on the side av the hill down the path to the shpring wid a crowbar, movin' a big shtone, an' the shweat rollin' in shtrames aff his face.

"'God save ye,' says Finn to him.

"'God save ye kindly,' says he to Finn.

"'It 's a bizzy man ye are,' says Finn.

"'Thrue for ye,' says the ditcher. 'It 's along o' the owld woman. "The way to the shpring is too stape an' shtoney," says she to me, an' sure, I 'm afther makin' it aisey for her.'

"'Ye 're the kind av a man to have,' says Missis Finn, shpakin' up. 'Sure all wimmin is n't blessed like your wife,' says she, lookin' at Finn, who let on to laugh when he wanted to shwear. They had some more discoorse, thin Finn an' his wife wint on, but it put a big notion into her head. If the bogthrotter, that was only a little ottommy, 'ud go to work like that an' make an aisey path for his owld woman to the shpring, phat 's the rayzon Finn cud n't fall to an' dig a path through the mountains, so she cud go to the say an' to the church on the shore widout breakin' her back climbin' up an' then agin climbin' down. 'T was the biggest consate iver in the head av her, an' she was n't wan o' thim that 'ud let it cool aff for the want o' talkin' about it, so she up an' towld it to Finn, an' got afther him to do it. Finn was n't aiger for to thry, bekase it was Satan's own job, so he held out agin all her scholdin' an' beggin' an' cryin'. Then she got sick on him, wid her headache, an' wint to bed, an' whin Finn was

about she 'd wondher out loud phat she was iver born for an'
why she cud n't die.   Then she 'd pray, so as Finn 'ud hear
her, to all the saints to watch over her big gossoon av a husband an' not forget him just bekase he was a baste, an' if Finn

'ud thry to quiet her, she 'd pray all the louder, an' tell him it
did n't matther, she was dyin' an' 'ud soon be rid av him an'
his brutal ways, so as Finn got half crazy wid her an' was
ready to do annything in the worruld for to get her quiet.

"Afther about a week av this thratemint, Finn give in an' wint to work wid a pick an' shpade on the Gray Man's Path. But thim that says he made it in wan night is ignerant, for I belave it tuk him a month at laste; if not more. So that's the thrue shtory av the Gray Man's Path, as me grandfather towld it, an' shows that a giont's size is n't a taste av help to him in a contist wid a woman's jaw.

"But to be fair wid her, I belave the onliest fault Finn's wife had was, she was possist be the divil, an' there's thim that thinks that's enough. I mind me av a young felly wan time that was in love, an' so to be axcused, that wished he'd a hunderd tongues so to do justice to his swateheart. So afther that he marr'd her, an' whin they'd been marr'd a while an' she'd got him undher her fisht, says they to him, 'An' how about yer hunderd tongues?' 'Begorra,' says he to thim agin, 'wid a hunderd I'd get along betther av coorse than wid wan, but to be ayquel to the waggin' av her jaw I'd nade a hunderd t'ousand.'

"So it's a consate I have that Missis Finn was not a haporth worse nor the rest o' thim, an' that's phat me grandfather said too, that had been marr'd twict, an' so knewn phat he was talkin' about. An' whin he towld the shtory av the Gray Man, he'd always end it wid a bit av poethry:—

> "'The first rib did bring in ruin
> As the rest have since been doin';
> Some be wan way, some another,
> Woman shtill is mischief's mother.

> "'Be she good or be she avil,
> Be she saint or be she divil,
> Shtill unaisey is his life
> That is marr'd wid a wife.'"

SATAN AS A SCULPTOR.

 one of the fishing villages which abound on the Clare coast, a narrow valley runs back from the sea into the mountains, opening between two precipices that, ages ago, were rent asunder by the forces of nature. On entering the valley by the road leading from the sea-shore, nothing can be seen but barren cliffs and craggy heights, covered here and there by patches of the moss peculiar to the country. After making some progress, the gorge narrows, the moss becomes denser on the overhanging rocks; trees, growing out of clefts in the precipices, unite their branches above the chasm, and shroud the depths, so that, save an hour or two at noon, the rays of the sun do not penetrate to the crystal brook, rippling along at the bottom over its bed of moss-covered pebbles, — now flashing white as it leaps down a declivity, now hiding itself under the overreaching ferns, now coming again into the light, but always hurrying on as though eager to escape from the dark, gloomy retreat, and, for a moment, enjoy the sunshine of the wider valley beyond before losing its life in the sea.

At a narrow turn in the valley and immediately over the spot where the brook has its origin in a spring bursting out of a crevice in the rock and falling into a circular well partly scooped out, partly built up for the reception of the sparkling water, a cliff rises perpendicularly to the height of fifty feet,

surmounted, after a break in the strata, by another, perhaps twenty feet higher, the upper portion being curiously wrought by nature's chisel into the shape of a human countenance. The forehead is shelving, the eyebrows heavy and menacing; the nose large and hooked like the beak of a hawk; the upper lip short, the chin prominent and pointed, while a thick growth of ferns in the shelter of the crag forming the nose gives the impression of a small mustache and goatee. Above the forehead a mass of tangled undergrowth and ferns bears a strong resemblance to an Oriental turban. An eye is plainly indicated by a bit of light-colored stone, and altogether the face has a sinister leer, that, in an ignorant age, might easily inspire the fears of a superstitious people.

On a level with the chin and to the right of the face is the mouth of a cave, reached by a path up the hillside, rude steps in the rock rendering easier the steep ascent. The cave can be entered only by stooping, but inside a room nearly seven feet high and about twelve feet square presents itself. Undoubtedly the cave was once the abode of an anchorite, for on each side of the entrance a Latin cross is deeply carved in the rock, while within, at the further side, and opposite the door, a block of stone four feet high was left for an altar. Above it, a shrine is hollowed out of the stone wall, and over the cavity is another cross, surmounted by the mystic I. H. S.

The legend of the cave was told by an old " wise woman " of the neighborhood with a minuteness of detail that rendered the narrative more tedious than graphic. A devout believer in the truth of her own story, she told it with wonderful earnestness, combining fluency of speech with the intonations of oratory in such a way as to render the legend as interesting as a dramatic recitation.

" 'T is the cave av the saint, but phat saint I 'm not rightly sartain. Some say it was Saint Patrick himself, but 't is I don't belave that same. More say it was the blessed Saint Kevin, him that done owld King O'Toole out av his land in the bargain he made fur curin' his goose, but that 's not thrue aither, an' it 's my consate they 're right that say it was Saint Tigernach, the same that built the big Abbey av Clones in Mona-

THE DEVIL'S FACE.   Page 175.

ghan. His Riverince, Father Murphy, says that same, an' sorra a wan has a chance av knowin' betther than him.

" An' the big head on the rock there is the divil's face that the saint made him put there, the time the blessed man was too shmart fur him whin the Avil Wan thried to do him.

" A quare owld shtory it is, an' the quol'ty that come down here on the coast laugh if it's towld thim, an' say it's a t'underin' big lie that's in it, bekase they don't undhershtand it, but if men belaved nothin' they did n't undhershtand, it's a short craydo they'd have. But I was afther tellin', Saint Tigernach lived in the cave, it bein' him an' no other; morebetoken, he was a good man an' shrewder than a fox. He made the cave fur himself an' lived there, an' ivery day he'd say tin thousand paters, an' five thousand aves, an' a thousand craydos, an' thin go out among the poor. There was n't manny poor thin in Ireland, Glory be to God, fur the times was betther thin, but phat there was looked up to the saint, fur he was as good as a cupboard to thim, an' whin he begged fur the poor, sorra a man 'ud get from him till he'd given him a copper or more, fur he'd shtick like a consthable to ye till he'd get his money. An' all that were parshecuted, an' the hungry, an' naked, and God's poor, wint to the saint like a child to its mother an' towld him the whole o' their heart.

" While the blessed saint lived here, over acrass the hill an' beyant the peat-bog there was a hedger an' ditcher named O'Connor. He was only a poor laborin' man, an' the owld woman helped him, while his girl, be the name o' Kathleen, tinded the house, fur I must tell ye, they kept a boord in the corner beways av a bar an' a jug wid potheen that they sowld to thim that passed, fur it was afore the days av the gaugers, bad cess to thim, an' ivery man dhrunk phat he plazed widout payin' a pinny to the govermint. So O'Connor made the potheen himself an' Kathleen sowld it to the turf-cutters, an' mighty little did they buy, bekase they 'd no money. She was a fine girl, wid a pair av eyes that 'ud dint the hearts av owld an' young, an' wid a dacint gown fur the week an' a clane wan fur the Sunday, an' just such a girl as 'ud make an owld felly feel himself young agin. Sorra the taste av divilmint was there in the girl at all, fur she was good as the sunshine in winther an' as innycent as a shpring lamb, an' wint to church an' did her jooty reglar.

"She was afther fallin' in love wid a young felly that done ditchin' an' they were to be marr'd whin he got his house done an' his father gev him a cow. He was n't rich be no manes, but as fur feelin' poverty, he never dhreamt o' such a thing, fur he 'd the love o' Kathleen an' thought it a forchune.

"In thim times the castle at the foot o' the hill was kept be a lord, that wid roomytisms an' panes in his jints was laid on his bed all the time, and the son av him, Lord Robert, was the worst man to be runnin' afther girls iver seen in the County Clare. He was the dandy among thim an' broke the hearts o' thim right an' lift like he was shnappin' twigs undher his feet. Manny a wan he desaved an' let go to the dogs, as they did at wanst, fur whin the divil gets his foot on a woman's neck, she niver lifts her head agin.

"Wan day, Lord Robert's father's roomytism got the bether av him an' laid him out, an' they gev him an iligant wake an' berryin', an' while they were at the grave Lord Robert looked up an' seen Kathleen shtandin' among the people an' wondhered who she was. So he come into the eshtate an' got a stable full av horses an' dogs, an' did a power o' huntin', an' as he was a sojer, he 'd a shwarm av throopers at the cassel, all the like av himself. But not long afther the berryin', Lord Robert was huntin' in the hills, an' he come down towards the bog an' seen O'Connor's cabin, an' says to his man, 'Bedad, I wondher if they 've a dhrop to shpare here, I 'm mortial dhry.' So in they wint, an' axed, an' got thim their dhrink, an' thin he set the wicked eyes av him on the girl an' at wanst remimbered her.

" ' It 's a mighty fine girl ye are,' says he to Kathleen thin, an' fit fur the house av a prince.'

" ' None o' yer deludherin' talk to me, Sorr,' says Kathleen to him. 'I know ye, an' it 's no good I know av ye,' says she to him. 'T was the good girl she was an' as firm as a land-lord in a bad year when she thought there was anny avil in-tinded.

" So he wint away that time an' come agin an' agin when he was huntin' an' always had some impidince to say at her. She towld her parrents av it, an' though they did n't like it at all, they was n't afeared fur the girl, an' he 'd spind more in wan dhrinkin' than they 'd take in in a week, so they were not sorry to see him come, but ivery time he come he wint away more detarmined to have the girl, an' whin he found he cud n't get her be fair manes he shwore he 'd do it be foul. So wanst, whin she 'd been cowlder to him than common an' would n't have a prisint he brought her, he says to her, 'Be-gob, I 'll bring ye to terms. If ye won't accept me prisints, I 'll make ye bend yer will widout prisints,' an' he wint away. She got frighted, an' whin she saw Tim Maccarty, she towld him av Lord Robert an' phat he said. Well, it made Tim mighty mad. 'Tatther an' agers,' says he, 'be the powers, I 'll break every bone in his body if he lays a finger on yer showldher; but, fur all that, whin Tim got to thinkin', he got skairt av Kathleen.

" ' Sure,' says he to himself, 'ain't wimmin like glass jugs, that 'll break wid the laste touch? I 'll marry her immejitly

an' take out av Clare into Kerry,' says he, 'an' let him dare
to come afther her there,' says he, for he knewn that if Lord
Robert came into the Kerry mountains, the boys 'ud crack his
shkull wid the same compuncshusness that they 'd have to an
egg shell.   So he left aff the job an' convaynienced himself to
go to Kathleen that night an' tell her his belafe.

"'Am n't I afeared fur ye, me darlin',' says he, 'and
would n't I dhrownd me in the say if anny harm 'ud come to
ye, so I think we 'd betther be married at wanst.'

" So Kathleen consinted an' made a bundle av her Sunday
gown, an' they shtarted fur the saint's cave, that bein' the
nearest place they cud be marr'd at, an' bein' marr'd be him
was like bein' marr'd be a priest.

" So they wint alang the road to where the foot-path laves
it be the oak-tree, then up the path an' through the boreen to
where Misther Dawson's black mare broke her leg jumpin' the
hedge, an' whin they rached that shpot they heard a noise on
the road behint thim an' stud be the hedge, peepin' through
to have a look at it an' see phat it was.   An' there was Lord
Robert an' a dozen av his bad min, wid their waypons an' the
armor on thim shinin' in the moonlight.   It was ridin' to
O'Connor's they were, an' whin Tim an' Kathleen set their eyes
on thim, they seen they 'd made a narrer eshcape.

" Howandiver, as soon as Lord Robert an' his min were out
o' sight, they ran wid all their shpeed, an' lavin' the path where
Dennis Murphy fell into the shtrame lasht winter comin' back
from Blanigan's wake whin he 'd had too much, they tuk the
rise o' the hill, an' that was a mishtake.   If they 'd kep be
the hedge an' 'round be the foot-bridge, then up the footway
the other side o' the brook an' ferninst the mill, they 'd have
kep out o' sight, an' been safe enough ; but as they were
crassin' the hill, wan av Robert's min saw thim, fur it was af-

ther the girl he was sure enough, an' whin he found from her father her an' Tim were gone, they rode aff here an' there sarchin' afther thim. Whin the sojer shpied thim on the top o' the hill, he blew his thrumpet, an' here come all the rest shtreelin' along on the run, round the hill as fast as their bastes 'ud take thim, fur they guessed where the two 'ud be goin'. An' Kathleen an' Tim come tumblin' down the shlope, an' bad luck to the minnit they 'd to shpare whin they got into the cave before here was the whole gang, wid their horses puffin', an' their armors rattlin' like a pedler's tins.

"The saint was on a pile av shtraw in the corner, shnorin' away out av his blessed nose, fur it was as sound aslape as a pig he was, bein' tired entirely wid a big day's job, an' did n't wake up wid their comin' in. So Lord Robert an' his min left their horses below an' climbed up an' looked in, but cud see nothin' be razon av the darkness.

"'Arrah now,' says he, 'Kathleen, come along out o' that now, fur I 've got ye safe an' sonnd.'

"They answered him niver a word, but he heard a noise that was the saint turnin' over on his bed bein' onaisey in his slape.

"'Come along out o' that,' he repaited; 'an' you, Tim Maccarty, if ye come out, ye may go back to yer ditchin', but if ye wait fur me to fetch ye, the crows 'ull be atin' ye at sunrise. Shtrike a light,' says he. So they did, an' looked in an' saw Tim an' Kathleen, wan on aitch side o' the althar, holdin' wid all their mights to the crass that was on it.

"'Dhrag thim out av it,' says Lord Robert, an' the min went in, but afore they come near thim, Saint Tigernach shtopped shnorin', bein' wakened wid the light an' jabberin', an' shtud up on the flure.

"'Howld on now,' says the blessed saint, 'phat 's the

matther here? Phat's all this murtherin' noise about?'
says he.

"Lord Robert's min all dhrew back, for there was a power
o' fear av the saint in the county, an' Lord Robert undhertuk
to axplain that the girl was a sarvint av his that run away wid

that thafe av a ditcher, but Saint Tigernach seen through the
whole thrick at wanst.

"'Lave aff,' says he. 'Don't offer fur to thrape thim lies
on me. Pack aff wid yer murtherers, or it's the curse ye'll
get afore ye can count yer fingers,' an' wid that all the min
went out, an' Lord Robert afther thim, an' all he cud say
'ud n't pervail on the sojers to go back afther the girl.

" ' No, yer Anner,' says they to him ; ' we ate yer Anner's mate, an' dhrink yer Anner's dhrink, an' 'ull do yer Anner's biddin' in all that 's right. We're parfectly willin' to wait till mornin' an' murther the ditcher an' shtale the girl whin they come out an' get away from the saint, but he mus n't find it out. It 's riskin' too much. Begorra, we 've got sowls to save,' says they, so they all got on their horses an' shtarted back to the cassel.

" Lord Robert folly'd thim a bit, but the avil heart av him was so set on Kathleen that he cud n't bear the thought av lettin' her go. So whin he got to the turn av the road, ' T'underation,' says he, ' 't is the wooden head that 's set on me showldhers, that I did n't think av the witch afore.'

" Ye see, in the break av the mountains beyant the mill, where the rath is, there was in thim times the cabin av a great witch. 'T was a dale av avil she done the County Clare wid shtorms an' rainy sayzons an' cows lavin' aff their milk, an' she 'd a been dhrownded long afore, but fur fear av the divil, her masther, that was at her elbow, whinever she 'd crook her finger. So to her Lord Robert wint, an' gev a rap on the dure, an' in. There she sat wid a row av black cats on aitch side, an' the full av a shkillet av sarpints a-shtewin' on the fire. He knew her well, fur she 'd done jobs fur him afore, so he made bowld to shtate his arriant widout so much as sayin' good day to ye. The owld fagot made a charm to call her masther, an' that minnit he was shtandin' be her side, bowin' an' schrapin' an' shmilin' like a gintleman come to tay. He an' Lord Robert fell to an' had a power av discoorse on the bargain, fur Robert was a sharp wan an' wanted the con- thract onsartain-like, hopin' to chate the divil at the end, as we all do, be the help av God, while Satan thried to make it shtronger than a tinant's lace. Afther a dale av palatherin', they aggrade that the divil was to do all that Lord Robert axed him fur twinty years, an' then to have him sowl an' body; but if he failed, there was an end av the bargain. But there was a long face on the owld felly whin the first thing he was bid to do was to bring Kathleen out o' the cave an' carry her to the cassel.

"'By Jayminny,' says Satan, 'it's no aisey job fur to be takin' her from the power av a great saint like him,' a-scratchin' his head. 'But come on, we'll thry.'

"So the three av thim mounted on the wan horse, Lord Robert in the saddle, the divil behind, an' the witch in front av him, an' away like the wind to the cave. Whin they got to the turn o' the hill, they got aff an' hid in the bushes be- chune the cave an' the shpring, bekase, as Satan axplained to Lord Robert, ivery night, just at midnight, the saint wint to get him a dhrink av wather, bein' dhry wid the devotions, an' 'ud bring the full av a bucket back wid him.

" ' We 'll shtop him be the shpring,' says the divil, ' wid the witch, an' you an' me 'ull shtale the girl while he 's talkin'.

" So while the clock was shtrikin' fur twilve, out come the saint wid the wather-bucket an' shtarted to the shpring. Whin he got there an' was takin' his dhrink, up comes the witch an' begins tellin' him av a son she had (she was purtindin', ye ondhershtand, an' lyin' to him) that was as lazy as a câr-horse an' as much in the way as a sore thumb, an' axin' the saint's advice phat to do wid him, while Satan an' Lord Robert ran into the cave. The divil picked up Kathleen in his arrums, but he dar n't have done that same, only she was on the other side av the cave an' away from the althar, but Tim was shtandin' by it, an' shtarted out wid her kickin' an' schraichin'. Tim ran to grip him, but Satan tossed him back like a ball an' he fell on the flure.

" ' Howld on till I shtick him,' says Lord Robert, pullin' out his soord.

" ' Come on, ye bosthoon,' says Satan to him. ' Sure the saint 'ull be on us if we don't get away quick,' an' bedad, as he said thim words, the dure opened, an' in come Saint Tigernach wid a bucket av wather on his arrum an' in a hurry, fur he misthrusted something.

" ' God's presince be about us,' says the blessed saint, whin he saw the divil, an' the turkey-bumps begun to raise on his blessed back an' the shweat a-comin' on his face, fur he knewn Satan well enough, an' consaved the owld felly had come fur himself be razon av a bit o' mate he ate that day, it bein' av a Friday ; axceptin' he did n't ate the mate but only tasted it an' then spit it out agin to settle a quarl bechune a butcher an' a woman that bought the mate an' said it was bad, only he was afeared Satan did n't see him when he sput it out

agin. 'God's presince be about us,' says the saint, a-crossin'
himself as fast as he cud. In a minnit though, he seen it
was n't him, but Kathleen, that was in it, an' let go the wather
an' caught the blessed crass that was hangin' on him wid his
right hand an' gripped Satan be the throat wid his lift, a-push-
in' the crass in his face.

"The divil dhropped Kathleen like it was a bag av male she
was, an' she rolled over an' over on the flure like a worrum
till she raiched the althar an' stuck to it as tight as the bark
on a tree. An' a fine thing it was to see the inimy av our
sowls a-lyin' there trimblin', wid the saint's fut on his neck.

"'Glory be to God,' says the saint. 'Lie you there till I
make an example av ye,' says he, an' turned to look fur Lord
Robert, bekase he knewn the two o' thim 'ud be in it. But
the Sassenagh naded no invitation to be walkin' aff wid himself, but whin he seen phat come to the divil, he run away
wid all the legs he had, an' the witch wid him, an' Tim afther
thim wid a whoop an' a fishtful av shtones. But they left
him complately an' got away disconsarted, an' Tim come back.

"'Raise up,' says Saint Tigernach to the divil, 'an' shtand
in the corner,' makin' the blessed sign on the ground afore
him. 'I 'm afther marryin' these two at wanst, widout fee or
license, an' you shall be the witness.'

"So he married thim there, while the divil looked on.
Faix, it 's no lie I 'm tellin' ye; it 's not the onliest marryin'
the divil 's been at, but he 's not aften seen at thim when he 's
in as low sper'ts as he was at that. But it was so that they
were married wid Satan fur a witness, an' some says the saint
thransported thim to Kerry through the air, but 't is n't meself
that belaves that same, but that they walked to Kilrush an'
wint to Kerry in a fisherman's boat.

"Afther they 'd shtarted, the saint turns to Satan an' says,

'No more av yer thricks wid them two, me fine felly, fur I mane to give you a job that'll kape ye out av mischief fur wan time at laste,' fur he was mightily vexed wid him a-comin' that-a-way right into his cave the same as if the place belonged to him.

"'Go you to work,' says he, 'an' put yer face on the rock over the shpring, so that as long as the mountain shtands min can come an' see phat sort av a dirthy lookin' baste ye are.'

"So Satan wint out an' looked up at the rock, shmilin', as fur to say that was no great matther, an' whin the blessed man seen the grin that was on him, he says, 'None av yer inchantmints will I have at all, at all. It's honest work ye'll do, an' be the same token, here's me own hammer an' chisel that ye'll take,' an' wid that the divil looked mighty sarious, an' left aff grinnin' for he parsaived the clift was granite.

"'Sure it's jokin' yer Riverince is,' says he, 'ye don't mane it. Sorra the harder bit av shtone bechuxt this an' Donegal,' an' it was thrue for him, fur he knewn the coast well.

"'Bad luck to the taste av a lie's in it,' says the saint. 'So take yer waypons an' go at it, owld Buck-an'-Whey, fur the sooner ye begin, the quicker ye'll be done, an' the shtone won't soften be yer watin'. Mind ye kape a civil tongue in yer head while ye're at the job, or it'll be a holiday to the wan I'll find ye,' says he, lookin' at him very fierce.

"So wid great displazemint, Satan tuk the hammer an' chisel, an' climbed up an' wint to work a cuttin' his own face on the shtone, an' it was as hard as iron it was, an whin he'd hit it a couple av cracks, he shtopped an' shuck his head an' thin scratched over his year wid the chisel an' looked round at the saint as fur to say somethin', but the blessed saint looked at him agin so fayroshus, that he made no raimark at all, but turned back to the clift quick an' begun to hammer

away in airnest till the shweat shtud on his haythenish face
like the dhrops on a wather-jug.

" On the next day, Lord Robert thought he 'd call the owld
Inimy, an' remind him that, bein' as he 'd failed to get Kathleen, their bargain was aff. So he made the charm Satan gev
him, but he did n't come fur anny thrial he 'd make.

" ' Bad scran to the Imp,' says he. ' Sure he must be
mighty busy or maybe he 's forgot entirely.'

" So he out an' wint to see the witch, but she was n 't in,
an' while he was waitin' for her, bein' not far away from the
saint's cave, he thought he 'd have a peep, an' see if Tim an'
Kathleen were shtill there. So he crawled over the top o' the
hill beyant the cave like the sarpint that he was, an' whin he
come down a little, he seen the owld Pooka on the clift, wid
the hammer in wan hand an' the chisel in the other a poundin'
away at the rock an' hangin' on be his tail to a tree. Lord
Robert thought the eyes 'ud lave his head, fur he seen it was
the divil sure enough, but he cud n't rightly make out phat he
was doin'. So he crawled down till he seen, an' thin, whin
he undhershtood, he riz an' come an' took a sate on a big
shtone ferninst the clift, a shlappin' his legs wid his hands, an'
roarin' an' the wather bilin' out av his eyes wid laughin'.

" ' Hilloo Nickey,' says he, when he 'd got his breath agin
an' cud shpake. ' Is it yerself that 's in it ? ' Mind the impidince av him, shpakin' that familiar to the inimy av our sowls,
but faix, he 'd a tongue like a jewsharp, an' cud use it too.

" ' Kape from me,' says Satan to him agin, as crass as two
shticks, an' widout turnin' his head fur to raigârd him. ' Lave
me ! Begorra, I 'll wipe the clift aff wid yer carkidge if ye
come anny closter,' says he.

" ' A-a-a-h, woorroo, now. Aisey, ye desayvin' owld blaggârd,' says Lord Robert, as bowld as a ram, fur he knewn

that Satan daren't lave the job to come at him. 'Will ye
kape yer timper? Sure ye haven't the manners av a goat, to
be shpakin' to a gintleman like that. I've just come to tell
ye that bein' ye failed, our bargain's aff,' says he.

" 'Out wid ye,' says the divil, turnin' half round an' howldin'
be wan hand to the big shtone nose he'd just done, an' shakin'
the other fist wid the chisel in it at Lord Robert. 'D' ye think
I want to be aggervated wid the likes av ye, ye whey-faced
shpalpeen, an' me losin' the whole day, an' business pressin'
at this saison, an' breakin' me back on the job, an' me fingers
sore wid the chisel, an' me tail shkinned wid howldin' on?
Bad luck to the shtone, it's harder than a Scotchman's head,
it is, so it is,' says he, turnin' back agin when he seen the
saint at the dure av the cave. An' thin he begun a peckin'
away at the clift fur dear life, shwearin' to himself, so the
saint cudn't hear him, every time he give his knuckles an onlucky crack wid the hammer.

" 'Ye 're not worth the throuble,' says he to Lord Robert;
he was that full av rage he cudn't howld in. 'It 's a pal-
therin' gossoon I was fur thriflin' wid ye whin I was sure av
ye annyhow.'

" 'Yer a liar,' says Lord Robert, 'ye desaivin' nagurly Haythen. If ye was sure o' me phat did ye want to make a bargain fur?'

" 'Yer another,' says Satan. 'Isn't a sparrer in yer hand
betther than a goose on a shtring?'

" So they were goin' on wid the blaggàrdin' match, whin
the blessed saint, that come out whin he heard thim begin, an'
thin set on the dure a-watchin', to see that owld Nick didn't
schamp the job, interfared.

" 'Howld yer pace, Satan, an' kape at yer work,' says he.
'An' for you, ye blatherin', milk-faced villin, wid the heart as

black as a crow, walk aff wid ye an' go down on yer hard-hearted onbelavin' knees, or it's no good 'ull come o' ye.' An' so he did.

"Do I belave the shtory? Troth, I dunno. It's quare things happened in them owld days, an' there's the face on the clift as ugly as the divil cud be an' the hammer an' chisel are in the church an' phat betther proof cud ye ax?

"Phat come av the lovers? No more do I know that, bar-rin' they grew owld an' shtayed poor an' forgot the shpring-time av youth in the winter av age, but if they lived a hun-derd years, they niver forgot the marryin' in the saint's cave, wid the black face av the Avil Wan lookin' on from the dark corner."

THE DEFEAT OF THE WIDOWS.

HEN superstitions have not yet been banished from any other part of the world it is not wonderful that they should still be found in the country districts of Ireland, rural life being especially favorable to the perpetuation of old ways of living and modes of thought, since in an agricultural district less change takes place in a century than may, in a city, be observed in a single decade. Country people preserve their old legends with their antique styles of apparel, and thus the relics of the pagan ages of Ireland have come down from father to son, altered and adapted to the changes in the country and its population. Thus, for instance, the old-fashioned witch is no longer found in any part of Ireland, her memory lingering only as a tradition, but her modern successor is frequently met with, and in many parishes a retired hovel in a secluded lane is a favorite resort of the neighboring peasants, for it is the home of the Pishogue, or wise woman, who collects herbs, and, in her way, doctors her patients, sometimes with simple medicinal remedies, sometimes with charms, according to their gullibility and the nature of their ailments.

Not far from Ballinahinch, a fishing village on Birterbuy Bay, in the County Galway, and in the most lonely valley of the neighborhood, there dwells one of these wise women who supplant the ancient witches. The hovel which shelters her bears every indication of wretched poverty; the floor is mud, the smoke escapes through a hole in the thatch in default of a chimney; the bed is a scanty heap of straw in the corner, and two rude shelves, bearing a small assortment of cracked jars and broken bottles, constitute Moll's stock in trade.

The misery of her household surroundings, however, furnished to the minds of her patients no argument against the efficiency of her remedies, Moll being commonly believed to have "a power av goold," though no one had ever seen any portion thereof. But with all her reputed riches she had no fear of robbers, for "she could aisily do for thim did they but come as many as the shtraws in the thatch," and would-be robbers, no doubt understanding that fact, prudently consulted their own safety by staying away from the vicinity of her cabin.

"Owld Moll," as she was known, was a power in the parish, and her help was sought in many emergencies. Did a cow go dry, Moll knew the reason and might possibly remove the spell; if a baby fell ill, Moll had an explanation of its ailment, and could tell at a glance whether the little one was or was not affected by the evil eye of a secret enemy. If a pig was stolen, she was shrewd in her conjectures as to the direction its wrathful owner must take in the search. But her forte lay in bringing about love-matches. Many were the charms at her command for this purpose, and equally numerous the successes with which she was accredited. Some particulars of her doings in this direction were furnished by Jerry Magwire, a jolly car-man of Galway, who had himself been benefited by her services.

" Sure I was married meself be her manes," stated Jerry,
" an' this is the way it was. Forty-nine years ago come next
Mickelmas, I was a good-lookin' young felly, wid a nate cabin
on the road from Ballinasloe to Ballinamore, havin' a fine câr
an' a mare an' her colt, that was as good as two horses whin the
colt grew up. I was afther payin' coort to Dora O'Callighan,
that was the dawther av Misther O'Callighan that lived in the
County Galway, an', be the same token, was a fine man. In
thim times I used be comin' over here twict or three times a
year wid a bagman, commercial thraveller, you 'd call him, an'
I heard say av Owld Moll, an' she was n't owld thin, an' the
next time I come, I wint to her an' got an inchantmint. Faix,
some av it is gone from me, but I mind that I was to change
me garthers, an' tie on me thumb a bit o' bark she gev me, an'
go to the churchyard on Halloween, an' take the first chilla-
ca-pooka (snail) I found on a tombshtone, an' begob, it was
that same job that was like to be the death o' me, it bein' dark
an' I bendin' to look clost, a hare jumped in me face from undher the shtone. ' Jagers,' says I, an' me fallin' on me back
on the airth an' the life lavin' me. ' Presince o' God be about
me,' says I, for I knewn the inchantmint was n't right, no more
I ought n't to be at it, but the hare was skairt like meself an'
run, an' I found the shnail an' run too wid the shweat pourin'
aff me face in shtrames.

" So I put the shnail in a plate that I covered wid another,
an' av the Sunday, I opened it fur to see phat letters it writ,
an' bad luck to the wan o' thim cud I rade at all, fur in thim
days I cud n't tell A from any other letther. I tuk the plate
to Misther O'Callighan, fur he was a fine scholar an' cud rade
both books an' writin', an' axed him phat the letters was.

" ' A-a-ah, ye ignerant gommoch,' says he to me, ' yer
head 's as empty as a drum. Sure here 's no writin' at all,

only marks that the shnail's afther makin' an' it crawlin' on the plate.'

"So I axplained the inchantmint to him, an' he looked a little closter, an' thin jumped wid shurprise.

"'Oh,' says he. 'Is that thrue?' says he. 'Ye must axqueeze me, Misther Magwire. Sure the shnails does n't write a good hand, an' I 'm an owld man an' me eyes dim, but I see it betther now. Faith, the first letter 's a D,' says he, an' thin he shtudied awhile. 'An' the next is a O, an' thin there 's a C,' says he, 'only the D an' the C is bigger than the O, an' that 's all the letters there is,' says he.

"'An' phat does thim letters shpell?' says I, bekase I did n't know.

"'Ah, bad scran to 'em,' says he; 'there 's thim cows in me field agin,' says he. 'Ax Dora, here she comes,' an' away he wint as she come in, an' I axed her phat D. O. C. shpelt; an' she towld me her name, an' I go bail she was surprised to find the shnail had writ thim letters on the plate, so we marr'd the next Sunday.

"But Owld Moll is a knowledgeable woman an' has a power av shpells an' charms. There 's Tim Gallagher, him as dhrives the public câr out o' Galway, he 's bought his luck av her be the month, fur nigh on twinty year, barrin' wan month, that he forgot, an' that time he shpilt his load in the ditch an' kilt a horse, bein' too dhrunk to dhrive.

"Whin me dawther Dora, that was named afther her mother, was ill afther she 'd been to the dance, whin O'Hoolighan's Peggy was married to Paddy Noonan (she danced too hard in the cabin an' come home in the rain), me owld woman wint to Moll an' found that Dora had been cast wid an avil eye. So she gev her a tay to dhrink an' a charm to wear agin it, an' afther she 'd dhrunk the tay an' put on the charm the faver lift her, an' she was well entirely.

"AN' PHAT DOES THIM LETTERS SHPELL?" Page 192.

" Sure Moll towld me wan magpie manes sorrow, two manes luck, three manes a weddin', an' four manes death ; an' did n't I see four o' thim the day o' the fair in Ennis whin O'Dougherty was laid out ? An' whin O'Riley cut his arrum wid a bill-hook, an' the blood was runnin', did n't she tie a shtring on the arrum an' dip a raven's feather into the blood av a black cat's tail, an' shtop the bleedin' ? An' did n't she bid me take care o' meself the day I met a red-headed woman afore dinner, an' it was n't six months till I met the woman in the mornin', it a-rainin' an' ivery dhrop the full o' yer hat, an' me top-coat at home, an' that same night was I tuk wid the roomytics an' did n't shtir a toe fur a fortnight. Faix, she 's an owld wan is Moll ; phat she can't do is n't worth thryin'. If she goes fur to make a match, all the fathers in Ireland cud n't purvint it, an' it 's no use o' their settin' theirselves agin her, fur her head 's as long as a summer day an' as hard as a shillalee.

" Did iver ye hear how she got a husband for owld Miss Rooney, the same that married Misther Dooley that kapes the Aygle Inn in Lisdoon Varna, an' tuk him clane away from the Widdy Mulligan an' two more widdys that were comin' down upon him like kites on a young rabbit ?

" Well, it 's a mighty improvin' shtory, fur it shows that widdys can be baten whin they 're afther a husband, that some does n't belave, but they do say it takes a witch, the divil, an' an owld maid to do it, an' some think that all o' thim is n't aiquel to a widdy, aven if there 's three o' thim an' but wan av her.

" The razon av it is this. Widdy wimmin are like lobsthers, whin they wanst ketch holt, begob, they 've no consate av lettin' go at all, but will shtick to ye tighter than a toe-nail, till ye 've aither to marry thim or murther thim, that 's the wan thing in the end ; fur if ye marry thim ye 're talked to

death, an' if ye murther thim ye 're only dacintly hanged out
o' the front dure o' the jail. Whin they 're afther a husband,
they 're as busy as owld Nick, an' as much in airnest as a dog
in purshoot av a flea. More-be-token, they 're always lookin'
fur the proper man, an' if they see wan that they think will
shuit, bedad, they go afther him as strait as an arrer, an' if
he does n't take the alarum an' run like a shape-thief, the
widdy 'ull have him afore the althar an' married fast an' tight
while he 'd be sayin' a Craydo.

"They know so much be wan axpayrience av marryin',
that, barrin' it 's a widdy man that 's in it, an' he knows as
much as thimselves, they 'll do for him at wanst, bekase it 's
well undhershtood that a bach'ler, aither young or owld, has
as much show av outshtrappin' a widdy as a mouse agin a weasel.

"Now, this Misther Dooley was an owld bach'ler, nigh on
five an' thirty, an' about fifteen years ago, come next Ad-
vint, he come from Cork wid a bit o' money, an' tuk the farm
beyant Misther McCoole's on the lift as ye come out o' Galway. He was n't a bad lookin' felly, an' liked the ladies, an'
the first time he was in chapel afther takin' the farm, aitch
widdy an' owld maid set the two eyes av her on him, an' the
Widdy Mulligan says to herself, says she, 'Faix, that 's just
the man to take the place av me dear Dinnis,' fur, ye see, the
widdys always do spake that-a-way av their husbands, a-givin'
thim the good word afther they 're dead, so as to make up fur
the tongue lashin's they give 'em whin they 're alive. It 's
quare, so it is, phat widdys are like. Whin ye see a widdy at
the wake schraimin' fit to shplit yer head wid the noise, an'
flingin' herself acrass the grave at the berryin' like it was a
bag o' male she was, an' thin spakin' all the time av 'me poor
dear hushband,' I go bail they lived together as paceful as a
barrel full o' cats an' dogs; no more is it sorrow that 's in it,

but raimorse that's tarin' at her, an' the shquailin' an' kickin'
is beways av a pinnance fur the gostherin' she done him whin
he was livin', fur the more there's in a jug, the less noise it

makes runnin' out, an' whin ye 've a heavy load to carry, ye
nade all yer breath, an' so have none to waste tellin' how it 's
breakin' yer back.

"So it was wid the Widdy Mulligan, that kept the Sham-

rock Inn, for her Dinnis was a little ottomy av a gossoon, an'
her the full av a dure, an' the arrum on her like a smith an'
the fut like a leg o' mutton.   Och, she was big enough thin,
but she 's a horse entirely now, wid the walk av a duck, an'
the cheeks av her shakin' like a bowl av shtirabout whin she
goes.   Her poor Dinnis dar n't say his sowl belonged to him,

but was conthrolled be her, an' they do say his last words
were, ' I 'll have pace,' that was phat he niver had afther he
married her, fur she was wan that 'ud be shmilin' an' shmilin'
an' the tongue av her like a razer.   She 'd a good bit o' property in the inn, siven beds in the house fur thravellers, an' six
childher, the oldest nigh onto twelve, an' from him on down
in reg'lar steps like thim in front o' the coort-house.

" Now, a bit up the shtrate from the Shamrock there was a little shop kept be Missis O'Donnell, the widdy av Tim O'Donnell, that died o' bein' mortified in his legs that broke be his fallin' aff his horse wan night whin he was comin' back from

Athlone, where he 'd been to a fair. Missis O'Donnell was a wapin' widdy, that 's got eyes like a hydrant, where ye can turn on the wather whin ye plaze. Begorra, thim 's the widdys that 'ull do fur anny man, fur no more can ye tell phat 's

in their minds be lookin' at their faces than phat kind av close they 've got on be lookin' at their shadders, an' whin they corner a man that 's tinder-hearted, an' give a shy look at him up out o' their eyes, an' thin look down an' sind two or three dhrops o' wather from undher their eye-lashers, the only salvation fur him is to get up an' run like it was a bag o' gunpowdher she was. So Missis O'Donnell, whin she seen Misther Dooley, tuk the same notion into her head that the Widdy Mulligan did, fur she 'd two childher, a boy an' a gurrul, that were growin' up, an' the shop was n't payin' well.

"There was another widdy in it, the Widdy McMurthry, that aftherwards married a sargeant av the polis, an' lives in Limerick. She was wan o' thim frishky widdys that shtruts an' wears fine close an' puts on more airs than a paycock. She was a fine-lookin' woman thim times, an' had money in plinty that she got be marryin' McMurthry, that was owld enough to be a father to her an' died o' dhrinkin' too much whishkey at first, an' thin too much sulphur-wather at Lisdoon Varna to set him right agin. She was always ready wid an answer to ye, fur it was quick witted she was, wid slathers o' talk that did n't mane annything, an' a giggle that she did n't nade to hunt fur whin she wanted it to make a show wid. An' she 'd a dawther that was a fine child, about siventeen, a good dale like her mother.

"Now, Misther Dooley had a kind heart in his body fur wimmin in gineral, an' as he liked a bit o' chaff wid thim on all occashuns, he was n't long in gettin' acquainted wid all the wimmin o' the parish, an' was well liked be thim, an', be the same token, was n't be the men, fur men, be nacher, does n't like a woman's man anny more than wimmin like a men's woman. But, afther a bit, he begun to centher himself on the three widdys, an' sorra the day' ud go by whin he come to town but phat he'd give wan or another o' thim a pace av his comp'ny that was very plazin' to thim. Bedad, he done that same very well, for he made a round av it for to kape thim in suspince. He'd set in the ale room o' the Shamrock an hour in the afthernoon an' chat wid the Widdy Mulligan as she was sarvin' the dhrink, an' shtop in the Widdy O'Donnell's shop as he was goin' by, to get a thrifle or a bit av shwates an' give to her childher beways av a complimint, an' thin go to Missis Mc-Murthry's to tay, an' so got on well wid thim all. An' it's me belafe he'd be doin' that same to this blessed day only that the widdys begun to be pressin' as not likin' fur to wait anny longer. Fur, mind ye, a widdy's not like a young wan that'll wait fur ye to spake, an' if ye don't do it, 'ull go on foriver, or till she gets tired av waitin' an' takes some wan else that does spake, widout sayin' a word to ye at all; but the widdy 'ull be hintin' an' hintin', an' her hints 'ull be as shtrong as a donkey's kick, so that the head o' ye has to be harder than a pavin'-shtone if ye don't undhershtand, an' ye've got to have more impidince than a monkey if ye don't spake up an' say something about marryin'.

"Well, as I was afther sayin', the widdys begun to be pressin' him clost: the Widdy Mulligan tellin' him how good her business was an' phat a savin' there'd be if a farm an' a public were put together; the Widdy O'Donnell a-lookin' at him out av her tears an' sighin' an' tellin' him how lonely he must be out on a farm an' nobody but a man wid him in the house, fur she was lonesome in town, an' it wasn't natheral at all, so it wasn't, fur aither man or woman to be alone; an' the Widdy McMurthry a palatherin' to him that if he'd a fine, good-lookin' woman that loved him, he'd be a betther man an' a changed man entirely. So they wint on, the widdys a-comin' at him, an' he thryin' to kape wid thim all, as he might have

knewn he could n't do (barrin' he married the three o' thim
like a Turk), until aitch wan got to undhershtand, be phat he
said to her, that he was goin' to marry her, an' the minnit
they got this in their heads, aitch begged him that he 'd shtay
away from the other two, fur aitch knewn he wint to see thim
all.   By jayminy, it bothered him thin, fur he liked to talk to
thim all aiquelly, an' did n't want to confine his agrayble
comp'ny to anny wan o' thim.   So he got out av it thish-a-way.
He promised the Widdy McMurthry that he 'd not go to the
Shamrock more than wanst in the week, nor into the Widdy
O'Donnell's barrin' he naded salt fur his cow; an' said to the
Widdy Mulligan that he 'd not more than spake to Missis
O'Donnell whin he wint in, an' that he 'd go no more at all
to Missis McMurthry's; an' he towld Missis O'Donnell that
whin he wint to the Shamrock he 'd get his sup an' thin lave
at wanst, an' not go to the Widdy McMurthry's axceptin'
whin his horse wanted to be shod, the blacksmith's bein' ferninst her dure that it 'ud be convaynient fur him to wait at.
So he shmiled wid himself thinkin' he 'd done thim complately, an' made up his mind that whin his pitaties were dug
he 'd give up the farm an' get over into County Clare, away
from the widdys.

   " But thim that think widdys are fools are desaved entirely,
an' so was Misther Dooley, fur instead av his throubles bein'
inded, begob, they were just begun.   Ivery time he wint into
the Shamrock Missis O'Donnell heard av it an' raymonshtrated
wid him, an' 'ud cry at him beways it was dhrinkin' himself to
death he was; afther lavin' the Shamrock, the Widdy Mulligan 'ud set wan av her boys to watch him up the strate an'
see if he shtopped in the shop.   Av coorse he cud n't go by,
an' whin he come agin, the Widdy Mulligan 'ud gosther him
about it, an' thin he 'd promise not to do it agin.   No more

cud he go in the Widdy O'Donnell's shop widout meetin' Missis McMurthry's dawther that was always shtreelin' on the strate, an' thin her mother 'ud say to him it was a power o' salt his cow was atin', an' the Widdy O'Donnell towld him his horse must be an axpensive baste fur to nade so much shooin'.

" Thin he 'd tell thim a lot o' lies that they purtinded to belave an' did n't, bekase they 're such desavers thimselves that it is n't aisey fur to do thim, but Dooley begun to think if it got anny hotter fur him he 'd lave the pitaties to the widdys to divide bechune thim as a raytribution fur the loss av himself, an' go to Clare widout delay.

" While he 'd this bother on him he got to know owld Miss Rooney, that lived wid her mother an' father on the farm next but wan to his own, but on the other side o' the way, an' the manes be which he got to know her was this. Wan mornin', whin Dooley's man, Paddy, wint to milk the cow, bad scran to the dhrop she 'd to shpare, an' he pullin' an' pullin', like it was ringin' the chapel bell he was, an' she kickin', an' no milk comin', faix not as much as 'ud blind the eye av a midge. So he wint an' towld Misther Dooley.

" ' I can get no milk,' says he. ' Begorra the cow 's as dhry as a fiddler's troat,' says he.

" ' Musha, thin,' says Misther Dooley, ' it 's the lazy omadhawn ye are. I don't belave it. Can ye milk at all ?' says he.

" ' I can,' says Paddy, ' as well as a calf,' says he. ' But phat 's the use ov pullin' ? Ye 'd get the same quantity from a rope,' says he.

" So Dooley wint out an' thried himself an' did n't get as much as a shmell of milk.

" ' Phat 's the matther wid the baste ?' says he, ' an' her on the grass from sun to sun.'

" ' Be jakers,' says Paddy, ' it 's my consate that she 's bewitched.'

" ' It 's thrue fur ye,' says Dooley, as the like was aften
knewn. ' Go you to Misther Rooney's wid the pail an' get
milk fur the calf, an' ax if there 's a Pishogue hereabouts.'

" So Paddy wint an' come back sayin' that the young lady
towld him there was.

" ' So there 's a young lady in it,' thinks Dooley. Faix, the
love av coortin' was shtrong on him. ' Did ye ax her how to
raich the woman ? '

" ' Bedad, I did n't. I forgot,' says Paddy.

" ' That 's yerself entirely,' says Dooley to him agin. ' I 'd
betther thrust me arriants to a four-legged jackass as to wan
wid two. He 'd go twict as fast an' remimber as much. I 'll
go meself,' says he, only wantin' an axcuse, an' so he did.
He found Miss Rooney thried to be plazin', an' it bein' convain-
ient, he wint agin, an' so it was ivery day whin he 'd go fur
the calf's milk he 'd have a chat wid her, an' sometimes come
over in the avenin', bekase it was n't healthy fur him in town
just thin.

" But he wint to Owld Moll about the cow, an' the charm
she gev him soon made the baste all right agin, but, be that
time, he 'd got used to goin' to Rooney's an' liked it betther
than the town, bekase whinever he wint to town he had to
make so many axcuses he was afeared the widdys 'ud ketch
him in a lie.

" So he shtayed at home most times and wint over to Rooney's the rest, fur it was n't a bad job at all, though she was
about one an' forty, an' had give up the fight fur a husband
an' so saiced strugglin'. As long as they 've anny hope, owld
maids are the most praypostherous craythers alive, fur they 'll
fit thimselves wid the thrappin's av a young gurrul an' look

as onaisey in thim as a boy wid his father's britches on. But
whin they 've consinted to the sitiwation an' saiced to struggle,
thin they begin to be happy an' enjoy life a bit, but there 's
no aise in the worruld fur thim till thin.   Now Miss Rooney
had gev up the contist an' plasthered her hair down on aitch
side av her face so smooth ye 'd shwear it was ironed it was,
an' begun to take the worruld aisey.

"But there 's thim that says an owld maid niver does give
up her hope, only lets on to be continted so as to lay in am-
boosh fur anny onsuspishus man that happens to shtray along,
an' faix, it looks that-a-way from phat I 'm goin' to tell ye,
bekase as soon as Misther Dooley begun to come over an' pa-
lather his fine talk to her an' say shwate things, thin she up
an' begins shtrugglin' harder nor iver, bekase it was afther
she 'd let go, an' comin' onexpected-like she thought it was a
dispinsation av Providence, whin rayly it was only an accident it was, beways av Dooley's cow goin' dhry an' the calf
too young to lave suckin' an' ate grass.

"Annyhow, wan day, afther Misther Dooley had talked
purty nice the avenin' afore, she put an her cloak, an' wint to
Owld Moll an' in an' shut the dure.

"'Now, Moll,' she says to the owld cuillean, ' it 's a long
time since I 've been to ye, barrin' the time the goat was lost,
fur, sure, I lost me confidince in ye.   Ye failed me twict,
wanst whin John McCune forgot me whin he wint to Derry
an' thin come back an' married that Mary O'Niel, the impidint young shtrap, wid the hair av her as red as a glowin'
coal ; an' wanst whin Misther McFinnigan walked aff from
me an' married the Widdy Bryan.   Now ye must do yer
besht, fur I 'm thinkin' that, wid a little industhry, I cud get
Misther Dooley, the same that the town widdys is so flus-
thrated wid.'

" ' An' does he come to see ye, at all ? ' says Moll.

" ' Faith he does, an' onless I 'm mishtaken is mightily plazed wid his comp'ny whin it 's me that 's in it,' says Miss Rooney.

" ' An' phat widdys is in it,' says Moll, as she did n't know, bekase sorra a step did the widdys go to her wid their love doin's, as they naded no help, an' cud thransact thim affairs thimselves as long as their tongues held out.

" So Miss Rooney towld her, an' Moll shuk her head. ' Jagers,' says she, ' I 'm afeared yer goose is cooked if all thim widdys is afther him.   I won't thry,' says she.

" But Miss Rooney was as much in airnest as the widdys, troth, I 'm thinkin', more, bekase she was fairly aitchin' fur a husband now she 'd got her mind on it.

" ' Sure, Moll,' says she, ' ye would n't desart me now an' it me last show. Thim widdys can marry who they plaze, bad scran to 'em, but if Misther Dooley gets from me, divil fly wid the husband I 'll get at all, at all,' beginnin' to cry.

" So, afther a dale av palatherin', Moll consinted to thry, bein' it was the third time Miss Rooney had been to her, besides, she wanted to save her charackther for a knowledgeable woman. So she aggrade to do her best, an' gev her a little bag to carry wid 'erbs in it, an' writ some words on two bits av paper an' the same in Latin. It was an awful charm, no more do I remimber it, fur it was niver towld me, nor to anny wan else, fur it was too dreadful to say axceptin' in Latin an' in a whisper fur fear the avil sper'ts 'ud hear it, that don't undhershtand thim dape langwidges.

" ' Now, darlint,' says owld Moll, a-givin' her wan, ' take you this charm an' kape it on you an' the bag besides, an' ye must manage so as this other paper 'ull be on Misther Dooley, an' if it fails an' he don't marry ye I 'll give ye back yer money an' charge ye nothing at all,' says she.

"So Miss Rooney tuk the charms an' paid Owld Moll one pound five, an' was to give her fifteen shillins more afther she was married to Dooley.

"She wint home, bothered entirely how she'd get the charm on Dooley, an' the avenin' come, an' he wid it, an' shtill she did n't know. So he set an' talked an' talked, an' by an' by he dhrunk up the rest av the whiskey an' wather in his glass an' got up to go.

"'Why, Misther Dooley,' says she, bein' all at wanst shtruck be an idee. 'Was iver the like seen av yer coat?' says she. 'Sure it's tore in the back. Sit you down agin wan minnit an' I'll mend it afore ye can light yer pipe. Take it aff,' says she.

"'Axqueeze me,' says Dooley. 'I may be a bigger fool than I look, or I may look a bigger fool than I am, but I know enough to kape the coat on me back whin I'm wid a lady,' says he.

"'Then take a sate an' I'll sow it on ye,' says she to him agin, so he set down afore the fire, an' she, wid a pair av shizzors an' a nadle, wint behind him an' at the coat. 'T was a sharp thrick av her, bekase she took the shizzors, an' whin she was lettin' on to cut aff the t'reads that she said were hangin', she ripped the collar, an' shlipped in the bit o' paper, an' sowed it up as nate as a samesthress in less than no time.

"'It's much beholden to ye I am,' says Dooley, risin' wid his pipe lit. 'An' it's a happy man I'd be if I'd a young woman av yer size to do the like to me ivery day.'

"'Glory be to God,' says Miss Rooney to herself, fur she thought the charm was beginnin' to work. But she says to him, 'Oh, it's talkin' ye are. A fine man like you can marry who he plazes.'

"So Dooley wint home, an' she, thinkin' the business as good as done, towld her mother that night she was to marry Misther Dooley. The owld lady cud n't contain herself or the saycret aither, so the next mornin' towld it to her sister, an' she to her dawther that wint to school wid Missis Mc-Murthry's gurrul. Av coorse the young wan cud n't howld her jaw anny more than the owld wans, an' up an' towld the wid-dy's dawther an' she her mother an' the rest o' the town, so be the next day ivery wan knew that Dooley was goin' to marry Miss Rooney: that shows, if ye want to shpread a bit o' news wid a quickness aiquel to the tellygraph, ye 've only to tell it to wan woman as a saycret.

"Well, me dear, the noise the widdys made 'ud shtun a dhrummer. Dooley had n't been in town fur a week, an' widdys bein' nacherly suspishus, they misthrusted that some-thin' was wrong, but divil a wan o' thim thought he 'd do such an onmannerly thrick as that. But they all belaved it, bekase widdys judge iverybody be themselves, so they were mighty mad.

"The Widdy McMurthry was first to hear the news, as her dawther towld her, an' she riz in a fury. 'Oh the ow-dashus villin,' says she; 'to think av him comin' here an' me listenin' at him that was lyin' fasther than a horse 'ud throt. But I 'll have justice, so I will, an' see if there 's law for a lone widdy. I 'll go to the judge,' fur, I forgot to tell ye, it was jail delivery an' the coort was settin' an' the judge down from Dublin wid a wig on him the size av a bar'l.

"Whin they towld Missis O'Donnell, she bust out cryin' an' says, 'Sure it can't be thrue. It is n't in him to desave a poor widdy wid only two childher, an' me thrustin' on him,' so she wint into the back room an' laid on the bed.

"But whin the Widdy Mulligan learned it, they thought

she 'd take a fit, the face av her got so red an' she chokin'
wid rage. 'Tatther an' agers,' says she. ' If I only had that
vagabone here five minnits, it 's a long day it 'ud be afore
he 'd desave another tinder-hearted faymale.'

" ' Oh, be aisey,' says wan to her, 'faix, you 're not the
onliest wan that 's in it. Sure there 's the Widdy O'Donnell an' Missis McMurthry that he 's desaved aiquelly wid
yerself.'

" ' Is that thrue ? ' says she; ' by this an' by that I 'll see
thim an' we 'll go to the judge an' have him in the prision.
Sure the Quane 's a widdy herself an' knows how it feels, an'
her judge 'ull take the part av widdys that 's misconshtrewed
be a nagurly blaggârd like owld Dooley. Bad luck to the
seed, breed, an' generation av him. I cud mop up the flure
wid him, the divil roast him, an' if I lay me hands on him, I 'll
do it,' says she, an' so she would; an' a blessing it was to Misther Dooley he was not in town just thin, but at home, diggin'
pitaties as fast as he cud, an' chucklin' to himself how he 'd
send the pitaties to town be Paddy, an' himself go to Clare
an' get away from the whole tribe av widdys an' owld
maids.

" So the Widdy Mulligan wint afther the Widdy O'Donnell
an' tuk her along, an' they towld thim av the Widdy McMurthry an' how she was done be him, an' they got her too, fur
they all said, ' Sure we would n't marry him fur him, but only
want to see him punished fur misconshtructing phat we
said to him an' lying to us.' Be this time half the town was
ready an' aiger to go wid thim to the coort, an' so they did,
an' in, wid the offishers thryin' to kape thim out, an' the wimmin shovin' in, an' all their frinds wid 'em, an' the shur'f
callin' out ' Ordher in the coort,' an' the judge lookin' over
his shpectacles at thim.

" ' Phat 's this at all ? ' says the judge, wid a solemnious voice. ' Is it a riat it is, or a faymale convulsion ? ' — whin he seen all the wimmin. ' Phat 's the matther ? ' says he, an' wid that all the wimmin begun at wanst, so as the noise av thim was aiquel to a 'viction.

" ' Marcy o' God,' says the judge, ' phat 's in the faymales at all ? Are they dishtracted entirely, or bewitched, or only dhrunk ? ' says he.

" ' We 're crazy wid graif, yer Lordshap,' they schraimed at him at wanst. ' It 's justice we want agin the uppresser.'

" ' Phat 's the uppresser been a-doin' ? ' axed the judge.

" ' Disthroyin' our pace, an' that av our families,' they said to him.

" ' Who is the uppresser ? ' he axed.

" ' Owld Dooley,' they all shouted at him at the wan time, like it was biddin' at an auction they were.

" So at first the judge cud n't undhershtand at all, till some wan whishpered the truth to him an' thin he scrotched his chin wid a pen.

" ' Is it a man fur to marry all thim widdys ? By me wig, he 's a bowld wan. Go an' fetch him,' he says to a consthable. ' Be sated, ladies, an' ye 'll have justice,' he says to the widdys, very p'lite. ' Turn out thim other blaggârds,' he says to the shur'f, an' away wint the polisman afther Dooley.

" He found him at home, wid his coat aff, an' him an' Paddy diggin' away at the pitaties for dear life, bekase he wanted to get thim done.

" ' Misther Dooley,' says the consthable to him, ' ye 're me prish'ner. Come along, ye must go wid me at wanst.'

" At first, Dooley was surprised in that degray he thought the life 'ud lave him, as the consthable come up behind him on the quiet, so as to give him no show to run away.

" ' Phat for ? ' says Dooley to him, whin he 'd got his wind agin.

" ' Faix, I 'm not sartain,' says the polisman, that was n't a bad felly ; ' but I belave it 's along o' thim widdys that are so fond o' ye. The three o' thim 's in the coort an' all the faymales in town, an' the judge sint me afther ye, an' ye must come at wanst, so make ready to go immejitly.'

" ' Don't go wid him,' says Paddy, wid his sleeves rowled up an' spitting in his hands. ' Lave me at him,' says he, but Dooley would n't, bekase he was a paceable man. But he was n't anxshus to go to the coort at all ; begob, he 'd all the coortin' he naded, but bein' there was no help fur it, he got his coat, the same that Miss Rooney sowed the charm in, an' shtarted wid the consthable.

" Now, it was that mornin' that owld Rooney was in town, thryin' to sell a goat he had, that gev him no end o' throuble be losin' itself part of the time an' the rest be jumpin' on the thatch an' stickin' its feet through. But he cud n't sell it, as ivery wan knew the baste as well as himself, an' so he was sober, that was n't common wid him. Whin he seen the widdys an' the other wimmin wid thim shtravigerin' through the strate on the way to the coort an' heard the phillaloo they were afther makin', he axed phat the matther was. So they towld him, an' says he, ' Be the powers, if it 's a question av makin' him marry some wan, me dawther has an inthrust in the matther,' so he dhropped the goat's shtring an' shtarted home in a lamplighter's throt to fetch her, an' got there about the time the polisman nabbed Dooley.

" ' There, they 're afther goin' now,' says he to her. ' Make haste, or we 'll lose thim,' an' aff they run, she wid her charm an' he widout his coat, grippin' a shillalee in his fisht, an' caught up wid Paddy that was follerin' the polisman an' Dooley.

" So they jogged along, comfortable enough, the polisman an' Dooley in the lade, afther thim owld Rooney an' Paddy, blaggârdin' the consthable ivery fut o' the way, an' offerin' fur to bate him so as he would n't know himself be lookin' in the glass, an' Miss Rooney in the rare, wondherin' if the charm 'ud work right. But Dooley did n't let a word out av his jaw, as knowin' he 'd nade all his breath afther gettin' into the coort.

" At the rise o' the hill the pursesshun was met be about a hunderd o' the town boys that come out fur to view thim, an' that yelled at Dooley how the widdys were waitin' to tare him in paces, an' that he was as good as a dead man a'ready, so he was; an' whin they got into town, all the men jined the show, roarin' wid laughter an' shoutin' at Dooley that the judge cud n't do anny more than hang him at wanst, an' to shtand it like a hayro, bekase they 'd all be at the hangin' an' come to the wake besides an' have a tundherin' big time. But he answered thim niver a word, so they all wint on to the coort, an' in, bringin' the other half o' the town wid 'em, the faymale half bein' there kapin' comp'ny wid the widdys.

" The minnit they come nie the dure, all the widdys an' wimmin begun in wan breath to make raimarks on thim.

" ' A-a-a-ah, the hang-dog face he has,' says Missis McMurthry. ' Sure has n't he the look av a shape-thief on the road to the gallus ? '

" ' See the haythen vagabone,' says the Widdy Mulligan. ' If I had me tin fingers on him for five minnits, it 's all the satiswhackshun I 'd ax. Bad cess to the hair I 'd lave on the head av him or in his whushkers aither.'

" But the Widdy O'Donnell only cried, an' all the wimmin turned their noses up whin they seen Miss Rooney comin' in.

" ' Look at that owld thing,' says they. ' Phat a power av

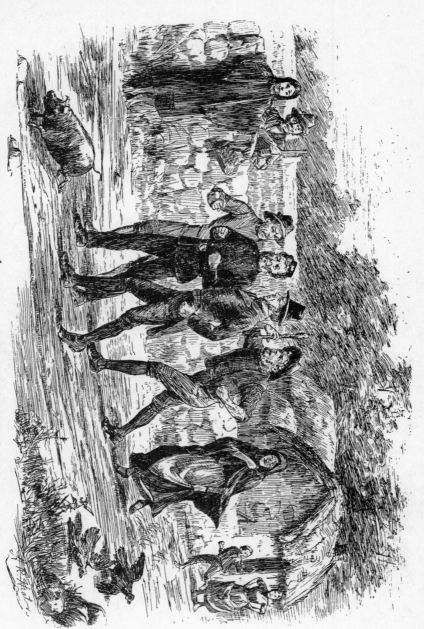

"OULD ROONEY AN' PADDY BLAGGÂRDIN' THE CONSTHABLE IVERY FUT O' THE WAY." Page 212.

impidince! Mind the consate av her to be comin' here wid him. Sure she has n't the shame av a shtone monkey,' says they av her.

" ' Silence in the coort,' says the shur'f. 'Stop that laughin' be the dure. Git along down out o' thim windys,' says he to the mob that Dooley an' the consthable brought wid thim.

" ' Misther Dooley,' says the judge, 'I 'm axed to b'lave ye 're thryin' to marry four wimmin at wanst, three av the same aforeshed bein' widdys an' the other wan not. Is it thrue, or do ye plade not guilty ?' says he.

" ' It 's not thrue, yer Lordshap,' says Dooley, shpakin' up, bekase he seen he was in for it an' put on a bowld face. ' Thim widdys is crazy to get a husband, an' misconsayved the manin' o' me words,' says he, an' that minnit you 'd think a faymale lunattic ashylum broke loose in the coort.

" They all gabbled at wanst like a field av crows. They said he was a haythen, a Toork, a vulgar shpalpeen, a lyin' blaggârd, a uppresser av the widdy, a robber av the orphin, he was worse than a nagur, he was, so he was, an' they niver thought av belavin' him, nor av marryin' him aither till he axed thim, an' so on.

" The judge was a married man himself an' knewn it was no use thryin' to shtop the gostherin,' for it was a joke av him to say that the differ bechuxt a woman an' a book was you cud shut up a book, so he let thim go on till they were spint an' out o' breath an' shtopped o' thimselves like an owld clock that 's run down.

" ' The sintince av this coort, Misther Dooley, is, that ye marry wan av 'em an' make compinsation to the other wans in a paycoonyary way be payin' thim siven poun' aitch.'

" ' Have marcy, yer Lordshap,' says Dooley, bekase he seen

himself shtripped av all he had. 'Make it five poun', an' that's more than I've got in money.'

"'Siven pound, not a haporth less,' says the judge. 'If ye have n't the money ye can pay it in projuice. An' make yer chice bechune the wimmin who ye'll marry, as it's married ye'll be this blessed day, bekase ye've gone too long a'ready,' says the judge, very starn, an' thin the widdys all got quite, an' begun to be sorry they gev him so many hard names.

"'Is it wan o' the widdys must I marry?' says Dooley, axin' the judge, an' the charm in his coller beginnin' to work hard an' remind him av Miss Rooney, that was settin' on wan side, trimblin'.

"'Tare an' 'ouns,' says the judge. 'Bad luck to ye, ye onmannerly idjit,' as he was gettin' vexed wid Dooley, that was shtandin', scrotchin' the head av him like he was thryin' to encourage his brains. 'Was n't it wan o' the wimmin that I tould ye to take?' says he.

"'If that's phat yer Lordshap says, axin' yer pardin an' not misdoubtin' ye, if it's plazin' to ye, bedad, I'll take the owld maid, bekase thim widdys have got a sight av young wans, an' childher are like toothpicks, ivery man wants his own an' not another felly's.' But he had another razon that he towld to me afther; says he, 'If I've got to have a famly, be jakers, I want to have the raisin' av it meself,' an' my blessin' on him for that same.

"But whin he was spakin' an' said he'd take Miss Rooney, wid that word she fainted away fur dead, an' was carried out o' the coort be her father an' Paddy.

"So it was settled, an' as Dooley did n't have the money, the widdys aggrade to take their pay some other way. The Widdy Mulligan tuk the pitaties he was diggin' whin the polisman gripped him, as she said they'd kape the inn all winter. The Widdy McMurthry got his hay, which come convaynient, bekase her brother kep post horses an' tuk the hay av her at two shillins undher the market. Missis O'Donnell got the cow that made all the throuble be goin' dhry at the wrong time, an' bein' it was a good cow was vally'd at tin poun'; so she gev him three poun', an' was to sind him the calf whin it was weaned. So the widdys were all paid for bein' wounded in their hearts be Misther Dooley, an' a good bargain they made av it, bekase a widdy's affections are like gârden weeds, the more ye thrample thim the fasther they grow.

"Misther Dooley got Miss Rooney, an' she a husband, fur they pulled her out av her faint wid a bucket o' wather, an' the last gossoon in town wint from the coort to the chapel wid Miss Rooney an' Misther Dooley, the latther crassin' himself ivery minnit an' blessin' God ivery step he tuk that it was n't the jail he was goin' to, an' they were married there wid a roarin' crowd waitin' in the strate fur to show thim home. But they sarcumvinted thim, bekase they wint out the back way an' through Father O'Donohue's gârden, an' so home, lavin' the mob howlin' before the chapel dure like wild Ingines.

"An' that's the way the owld maid defated three widdys, that is n't often done, no more would she have done it but for owld Moll an' the charm in Dooley's coat. But he's very well plazed, an' that I know, for afther me first wife died, her I was tellin' ye av, I got the roomytics in me back like tin t'ousand divils clawin' at me backbone, an' I made me mind up that I'd get another wife, bekase I wanted me back rubbed, sence it 'ull be chaper, says I, to marry some wan to rub it than to pay a boy to do that same. So I was lookin' roun' an' met Misther Dooley an' spake av it to him, an' good luck it 'ud

have been if I 'd tuk his advice, but I did n't, bein' surrounded
be a widdy afther, that 's rubbed me back well fur me only
wid a shtick.   But says he to me, ' Take you my advice Misther Magwire, an' whin ye marry, get you an owld maid, if
there 's wan to be had in the counthry.   Gurruls is flighty an'
axpectin' too much av ye, an' widdys is greedy buzzards as
ye 've seen be my axpayrience, but owld maids is humble, an'
thankful for gettin' a husband at all, God bless 'em, so they
shtrive to plaze an' do as ye bid thim widout grumblin' or
axin' throublesome questions.' "